"One of the most valued positions in the range of vocations is that of private or personal secretary. Few occupations require the versatility and skill exercised by men and women who function in this capacity."

BEGINNING WITH THE INTERVIEW, this important guide covers all aspects of a secretary's job. It is a complete, compact, all-purpose business reference book by a professional whose background has included personal service to some of America's most prominent businessmen. Here is authoritative, inside advice on how to give the most to, and get the most from your job . . . how to become an expert in an increasingly complex area of endeavor.

THE SECRETARY'S MANUAL

by J. H. Stroman

A SIGNET BOOK from
NEW AMERICAN LIBRARY
TIMES MIRROR

SIGNET, SIGNET CLASSICS, MENTOR, PLUME AND MERIDIAN BOOKS
are published by The New American Library, Inc.,
1301 Avenue of the Americas, New York, New York 10019

FIRST PRINTING, MAY, 1968

    4 5 6 7 8 9 10 11 12

PRINTED IN THE UNITED STATES OF AMERICA

Contents

THE
SECRETARY'S
MANUAL

Preface

One of the most valued positions in the range of vocations is that of private or personal secretary. Few occupations require the versatility and skill exercised by men and women who function in this capacity. Properly exacting and efficient persons, they realize their limitations and constantly strive to increase their knowledge and expand their personalities.

In the early part of this century it was recognized that a secretarial job was a good entrée into a large organization because it would lead to promotions. The secretary, exposed to confidential information, was given the opportunity to make himself or herself indispensable. That was, however, an era when the job of secretary had not attained its present recognition as an end in itself. Now many a secretary has quite as much responsibility and influence as formerly was wielded by a person in a more officially titled position.

In those days the rumor went, "There's no such thing as a good male secretary," for the reason that a man who could be a good secretary would soon advance into a higher bracket, the status of men not being limited. Nevertheless, today men frequently remain secretaries, undertaking difficult liaison and managerial tasks and even traveling with their employers as would not always be possible for women. A prime minister of England or a President of the United States needs the highest caliber person to relieve him of multiple burdens. Often a secretary has many assistants accomplishing his own detailed work, while he holds himself ready to represent his principal in executive matters.

The author, as a result of his long years of service as a secretary to prominent men and as a result of his contact with many of America's most successful secretaries, has here compiled vitally important suggestions for a secretary who must operate in the complicated business and professional world of today.

May *The Secretary's Manual* sharpen the interpretation of this exciting vocation in the minds of ambitious stenographers, self-improving secretaries, employers, supervisors, personnel directors, placement agents, vocational counselors, educators, and all students of twentieth-century office procedures.

—JAMES H. STROMAN

I

The General View

Why Is a Secretary?

A secretary is engaged by a busy employer because he needs someone to relieve him of a great deal of his work, especially the detail of office procedure and the handling of other matters that do not require his own expensive time. But everything she does for him must duplicate what he himself would do if he were not absorbed in transactions that cannot be delegated.

Every man dreams of having a perfect secretary, and every secretary dreams of becoming so well-adjusted to her employer that they will work as a team, each trusting the other to carry part of the load in harmony.

The Interview

When engaging a secretary, the employer considers whether the applicant is of a dependable character—whether she will conserve her health (even at the cost of forgoing a social event) in order always to be punctually on hand during office hours. He knows from experience that girls who periodically take sick leave are not interested in their work and he tries to ascertain the focus of the applicant's attention.

He will also consider her probable disposition, trying to judge whether she is the kind of person who rushes home at five o'clock regardless of the state of affairs in the office, or whether she can become personally involved to the point of volunteering to remain after hours if an emergency arises.

He will inquire about the extent of her education, not only for the sake of her answer to that question, but mainly in order to gauge her capacity for continuing to learn. An employer can discount whatever she does not know when she begins to work for him, if he believes she will apply herself and eventually accumulate the knowledge necessary for success.

There are two important qualities an employer must demand in a secretary. He can hardly discuss these, for the reason that they are either present or not and cannot be taught. Is the applicant, he asks himself, one who exercises loyalty? And can she realize the confidential nature of everything that passes through her hands, so that certain projects not ripe for public announcement will not have to be screened from her desk? In an office there is nothing more unwelcome than the "human sieve" who chatters about every conversation she hears.

For an intelligent employer, one interview will reveal many things about the prospective secretary besides her proficiency in taking dictation and transcribing it. He observes her quick-wittedness and her resilient moods; he decides whether her work is more important to her than her social commitments so that a sudden change in the lunch hour (for instance) will not arouse her resentment; he appraises the quality of her conversation, her courtesy, and her ease in establishing cordial relations with colleagues.

If the employer is satisfied on all these points, he will consider money paid to a secretary of far less value than her actual worth. Even then he may give himself leeway to surprise her with a raise in salary after a short period of adjustment and will therefore offer her less as a beginning salary than he is eventually willing to pay. Her treatment of this offer may turn out to be a test: Does she recognize the opportunities for promotion inherent in this position, or has she too little foresight?

Because the employer is looking for a secretary who will increase his own efficiency, he may back away from an applicant who is too aggressive. He may have had the experience of admiring a secretary's initiative until she too often explained why her way was best, unwittingly wasting his time. Though her interest is prized, he prefers not to argue points that he has already decided after due cogitation. He has things more important to do than to place before her all his reasons for pursuing a particular policy. He therefore tries to find a secretary who will execute his own plan no matter how many alternatives may be obvious.

In other words, the employer is in search of an efficient tool whose personality will be an asset instead of a handicap, who has natural loyalty, and whose ability to refrain from betraying confidences gives him a sense of security.

During the first interview it is wise for the applicant to be as natural and relaxed as possible, despite a tendency to be nervous at such a time. It is taken for granted that she has appeared dressed neatly and without flashiness, her hair well-groomed and her face inconspicuously made-up. She has been careful to satisfy herself about her appearance before leaving the mirror and can therefore forget for the moment what she looks like.

If she tries too hard to sell herself she may make a poor impression. She should allow the employer to make his own decision on what he can understand about her without trying to influence him, no matter how subtly. After all, he knows better than she does the kind of secretary he wants. He may have some subconscious quirk that makes him prefer to work with an entirely different type of person; in that case it is wiser for him to make another selection. Leaving all this to him is part of her respect for him, and it will win his respect for her whether or not he engages her.

The Apprenticeship

No matter how well-experienced a secretary is, when she begins a new job in a new office under a new employer she must be prepared to serve an apprenticeship. Her past is useful only inasmuch as it has taught her to learn quickly and to evaluate new situations. She will find that in the new office there is a new method for almost every daily process—even for opening and distributing the morning mail. There will no doubt be a filing system she has not used elsewhere and a way of typing letters that contrasts with her former employer's preference. Now she must use paragraphing and punctuation and abbreviations that were vetoed in her former connection. She will discover also that her new employer has a varied vocabulary not entirely familiar to her.

The new secretary should take time to study the files so that she will have advance knowledge of the projects under-way in this office. She should also keep alert to everything that happens and remain as flexible as a dancer—especially adjusting to the personalities around her. Whatever she has been accustomed to do heretofore is of no worth if it is contrary to the present requirements. She must fit into a new slot, must change many of her office habits, must keep in mind every minute that she is here to carry out the orders and the whims of an entirely new character—a boss who judges her only by the measure with which she suits his own long-ago-determined mannerisms.

The new secretary will not necessarily meet with hostility from her office associates, but she will find herself a stranger among them. Although they may be gracious, they will hard-ly forget that she is new and will have no interest in anything she has done earlier. Nothing can win their approbation except her acceptance of their own ways.

Only after this has been shown will she be "one of them" and thus be entitled to make a suggestion of her own once in a while. The thing for a new secretary to remember is that when she does have a suggestion to offer it may very well be one that has often been made before and been rejected for excellent reasons after heartfelt debate. If she will remain silent until she knows the regulations governing this new office, then she will save herself from what may look like gaucheries to those who have already been over the field.

Sometimes a new secretary decides to arrive at the office a few minutes late and to take liberties at the lunch hour, only to start a precedent: She wants to be recognized as some-body of importance. This is the worst possible mistake, and it ought not to be necessary to mention it here, in view of the fact that common sense would automatically tell one to avoid it; however, when we are young we can be protected by a timely word. In this situation the best way for the secretary to prove that she is somebody of importance is to show consideration for others "beyond the call of duty." A little extra giving will cost nothing but will bring big dividends in trust and friendship among the office personnel.

Once a stenographer who repeatedly went out of her way to serve others was lovingly referred to as Sourpuss—because it was understood by everybody in the office that she had the sweetest nature found in woman. Any member of the staff would have gone to great lengths to please her.

If you are getting along well with others in the office, your employer will feel that sense of security he has been hoping for: Here at last he has found the perfect secretary. Not only can she spell, type rapidly, and answer the phone with courtesy, but she can also be relied upon to keep relations harmonious.

Daily Routine

The first thing every morning, when you arrive at the office, air the rooms and regulate the heat, then arrange your desk for efficiency, replenishing your supplies. Prepare your notebook and pencils or pens for dictation so that, if your employer rings, you will not have to look here and there in haste for what you need. Every time you delay you are costing the employer valuable time.

Consult your desk calendar to be sure you are aware of all that you must do during the day. Check your list of recurring matters: board meetings, payroll dates, interest payments, renewal dates, and tax and insurance payments. Place on your employer's desk a typed schedule of his own appointments for the day and prepare for him any material from the file that he will need for these appointments.

If you have to speak with two or three callers, show your most pleasing manners and do what you can to help them. If they are not able to postpone their calls until a later date and your employer happens to be in conference, judge whether you consider this a matter of such importance that you ought to intrude into the conference room. If you do so, enter without knocking and go silently to your employer, handing him a typed memo about the caller who is waiting. He will decide if the caller ought to wait or if he does not care to give time to this particular caller. You can then obey his instruction and retire from the room without having disturbed anyone.

Sometimes when your employer is closeted with a caller he may touch a concealed bell as a signal for you to help him to close the interview. In that event you can look into his office and say very gently, "Mr. Brown, your next appointment is

for five minutes from now." The caller will realize it is time
for him to go.

Dictation

The new secretary ought to keep a notebook and pencil or
pen in some inconspicuous spot in her employer's private
office so that she will always be ready to take dictation, even
if she has merely looked in to announce a caller.

Each day when you begin dictation, first write the date at
the top of the notebook page. When the dictation comes to
an end you ought to write the date once more and draw a
line across the page. Though there may be several dictation
periods a day, you will find this helpful, if only in times of
emergency, for you will be able to refer to your notes rapidly
if some question arises.

When you have to take dictation from more than one
person, be sure to keep separate notebooks with the proper
names on the outside in a prominent place. If you are asked
a question about one of the letters, you will be able to reply
without hesitation, especially if you have remembered to
write the date before and after each session of dictation.

During the regular dictation the employer will often give
telegrams or other communications that ought to be sent out
promptly, though he may continue dictating for an hour or
more before the secretary can take care of them. In such an
event the secretary should, after taking the dictation of the
telegram or urgent letter, turn down the page in her notebook so that she can quickly refer to it as soon as she reaches
her typewriter.

Now and then, while the employer is marshaling his ideas
and dictating, he may make a remark that the secretary does
not hear distinctly, and it is then imperative that she ask him
to repeat it before he resumes. He will respect her accuracy
more than her fear to interrupt him.

When there are names of correspondents and companies
and products with which she is not acquainted, the secretary
should be sure to have explanatory papers given to her
before she allows herself to close that bit of dictation. Or she
should ask if these names are in the file and plan to refer to
the particular folder containing them when she begins to
transcribe her notes.

Transcription

When the material the secretary has taken in shorthand is unfamiliar to her and she has to delay overnight before transcribing the notes, she ought to take the time before going home to scan them and check to be sure that she will understand them the next day. Of course it is better that her shorthand be so reliable that she can count on reading it even after a lapse of years; just the same, there are instances when a few minutes' survey will save an hour's puzzling later.

During her transcription of the notes, a secretary ought always to allow herself to doubt a spelling now and then, rather than hastily type what may be an unacceptable form of a word. Where there is the slightest doubt she should refer to the dictionary. One girl retorted, "A dictionary is of no use unless you know how to spell the word." There is always someone in the office, however, who will welcome your inquiry and join you in finding the word in the dictionary if you do need assistance. This is a game that we can all play together, for all of us are continually learning to spell, all of us meeting words for the first time, regardless of the number of years we have been to school.

When the employer is well-read and well-traveled, when he daily converses with other brilliant men, he will naturally have an extensive vocabulary. The secretary should take every opportunity to improve her own vocabulary, day by day adding to her knowledge of her language—the implement by which she carves herself a place among cultivated persons. Nobody would expect to build a house before he learned to handle a hammer, and yet many a person talks incessantly without ever having learned to use his native language properly.

After you have transcribed your notes, be sure to read over what you have typed. If there is even one error it is better for you yourself to find it than to wait for somebody else to accost you with it later. Make a neat erasure and carefully fit the paper into your typewriter so that you can strike the right letter in exactly the right spot, not too heavily, and in the same type-color as the rest of the sheet. The pride that a correct page gives you will be one of your happy reasons for enjoying your job.

The Intangibles

If the secretary is patient with her employer's vagaries, he will become patient with her own lapses. She will excuse any of his faults if the job is worth holding, and he will excuse any of her faults if she gives exceptional service despite them.

She must exercise self-control every moment, even when her courtesy is strained. She is not living her personal life but is representing her employer, and she can never indulge in temperament or criticism of those around her. She must always think before she speaks, must keep herself open like an impersonal channel for the fulfillment of her role as secretary. Think of how a diplomat must act while he represents his country in a foreign land.

The secretary will soon learn whether her employer likes to have her dust his desk and straighten the papers on it. She may help by stacking the files he is consulting and replacing in the cabinet those he has already consulted. A great many little matters will be left unmentioned between her and her employer but will be important in her effort to be of maximum assistance to him. While they work together, a certain amount of telepathic connection will develop between them, so that their understanding of each other will enhance their success in the common task.

Discretion is necessary, for the secretary must not overstep certain bounds; she must avoid touching or mentioning papers that he considers personal and private to himself—at least until she has taught him that her only motive is service to him. He will trust her as soon as he learns that she cares more for the success of his work than for herself.

The secretary can make appointments for her employer and record them on his desk calendar or in any book he maintains for this purpose. She can also avoid making appointments for him that he does not favor. A great deal of tact will be essential in the latter instance, for only sympathy with the feelings of others will save her from offending. And there are times when a secretary will have to remind her employer of appointments so that he will not schedule too much work for himself on the morning when he must appear at a conference, let us say.

It has in the past been a matter of conjecture whether or not secretaries had to remind their bosses of a wife's birthday or other personal matters, but very few secretaries of really prominent men have ever had this duty. A man who is outstanding in his community is usually the kind of man who has his private life well in hand. If he is "friends" with his wife, she herself may be left to remind him as her birthday approaches; his secretary, moreover, is far too busy with office matters to interfere with his family life unless she is definitely instructed to do so.

Each good secretary will encounter her own problems in this and in other fields and will solve them as intelligently as she can, always remembering her role as personal assistant in every degree.

Aside from the writing of letters and reports and tabulations of progress that the secretary must prepare, there are telephone and telegraph communications, as well as teletype. Moreover, many personal contacts test the secretary's character as well as her judgment and memory. She must know exactly what her employer wants her to confide to the public and when she must gracefully reply, "I couldn't say." It is never necessary for her to tell a falsehood, for she will be dealing with persons who understand her position and who respect her for keeping a confidence. Often she will find it wisest to explain frankly that a particular bit of information is not for public consumption.

The secretary may make traveling arrangements for her employer, order lunch sent up to him and his colleagues when they are conferring in his office, or reserve a table at a hotel or club when he has a luncheon or dinner meeting. She will make his bank deposits and withdrawals and sometimes will deliver documents to the safe-deposit vault. She will make periodic payments on his insurance, taxes, and real estate investments and, at his instruction, will keep in touch with his broker. In all such matters she will govern herself according to his desires.

At times she will find it necessary to remain part of the evening to finish an emergency job. She ought to be wise enough, however, to explain to her employer when her burden is too heavy for her to do competently within the office hours, so that he may authorize her to take on a temporary assistant or to borrow an assistant from some other department. No secretary should risk her health showing "good old-fashioned self-sacrifice" in order to do more than is sensible for her to do, day after day over a long period. If she finds her work load too heavy, she may have to admit that she is incapable of doing it properly, or she may need a full-time assistant. Either possibility should be coped with as soon as it becomes obvious.

Sometimes common sense will save oppressive work. One girl, on assuming a job, was told to keep a chronological list of all incoming and outgoing letters with full analyses of their contents. She faithfully complied, though this necessitated her spending many evenings over it. More than a year later, she was demoted to another department. The girl who replaced her, on being told about this elephantine task, asked, "Haven't you always been able to hand him the letter from the file so that he could read it for himself without having to study your analysis?"

"So far, yes."

The new secretary saw that there was no use for the list and that it had been ordered through the employer's fear that the files would not be reliable. She discontinued it and was thus freed to do current work. Her employer congratulated her on the change she had made, never learning what had mired his former secretary.

Time-Savers

In most instances an overburdened secretary can be relieved by the installation of some modern time-saving devices.

Dictating machines are not always welcomed by a secretary who thinks of them as merely a new complication. But she will soon learn that they are designed for use with a minimum of skill on her part. They save her the doube job of taking dictation before transcription, and, while her employer is dictating at his leisure, she can finish tasks that previously had to be neglected under pressure of time.

When the employer possesses a portable dictating machine small enough to fit into an attaché case, he can get some of his dictation done at home or while traveling. After he delivers the recording (on tape, wire, disk, or belt) to his secretary, she will be able to transcribe it at her own convenience.

If you notice indications on the dictation machine card

that there are any corrections, take the time to listen to the letter before you begin to type it. You may save yourself a second typing by estimating the length before you begin to type it, especially if your employer failed to mark the end of the letter. In such a situation you may prefer to run off a rough draft instead of merely listening. Using a rough draft is also a good idea when you begin to transcribe for a new dictator, before your ear has become accustomed to his voice.

Some offices provide the secretary with a machine that slits open mail—another useful time-saver. Where the outgoing mail is heavy it is more important than ever for her to have a metering machine that folds the enclosure, inserts it in the envelope, seals the envelope, and stamps it at the same time. It used to be possible to hire young office boys for such menial tasks, but, now that the custom has changed, the secretary can use the machine for that work.

When there is a long mailing list to which announcements or other information must be sent regularly, an automatic envelope addresser can be used. A card or stencil for each address can be inserted with the envelopes, and the cards or stencils can be used repeatedly. There is another machine that actually affixes address labels to the envelopes, which might be closer to the requirements of some offices.

If you have to seal a large number of envelopes by hand, place them with the address down, the flaps opened in a fanlike formation, and the glued rims close together. With a moist sponge dampen several of the glued flaps with one long stroke. Then turn the flaps down, one at a time, pressing each following envelope upon the sealed one that preceded, thus assuring yourself that the sealing is firm.

When typing many envelopes or many cards, considerable time will be saved if you "chain-feed" them into the carriage: typing one while rolling the platen to displace the last, letting them pile up on the desk behind the typewriter until you are ready to gather them up for mailing.

Copying machines are needed in many industrial and publicity offices, though not in executive offices where officials use their secretaries for the development of policy. Just the same, the secretary ought to acquaint herself with the modern methods used in other departments, because she may at any time be able to improve her efficiency by recommending some time-saving device.

Some copiers operate by photography, making use of chemicals—but in such an efficient manner that there is no untidiness at the desk. After one copy is made the "negative" can be returned to the developer for making extra copies.

There is also the copier that produces in seconds black-on-white or color-coded copies by the use of the original plus one sheet of copy paper. And there is the heat process that requires no chemicals at all; an image is literally burned into special paper. Then there is the electrostatic process that gives you a copy (on special paper or on regular bond, letterhead, or office form) immediately after you place the original in the machine.

If your employer needs a thousand copies of one sheet or one copy of a blueprint, he will keep a duplicator in the office. There is also a new printing device made especially for postcards: it can reproduce handwritten messages as well as illustrations.

Microfilming has become essential in large organizations where the material required for consultation in the executive's office may be on file in a remote place in the plant. Besides, whereas a filing cabinet may be quickly overcrowded, microfilming can put twenty-five hundred letters on one hundred feet of film within a few seconds. The equipment includes a viewer so that the microfilmed material can be enlarged within a lighted area for one's perusal. The section you need can also be developed for your office use.

Perforated tape for automatic typewriters can be fed the code number of certain standard paragraphs used frequently in letters. Each such paragraph is numbered, and a set of corresponding numbers is on the control box for the typewriter. The secretary can then type the name and address of the addressee and push the buttons for the selected paragraphs, and the typewriter will finish the letter at one hundred words a minute. If there happen to be two such automatic typewriters in the office, the secretary can move from one to the other, keeping them both in production at the same time.

Social Amenities

When acting for her employer the secretary must follow established patterns of etiquette in all her office contacts and in speaking with callers. To smoothen the observance of the amenities in social exchanges, her full experience in this respect ought to be on file so that she may refer to past occurrences for guidance in new situations.

For formal occasions, fully engraved invitations are printed on plain heavy white or ivory paper with no address, initial, name, or monogram. The printer will have a book of samples and will make recommendations when taking the order. Partially engraved invitations that should be filled out by hand are used when the number of guests is not sufficient to warrant fully engraved invitations. Handwritten formal invitations are sent on smooth, heavy, fold-over cards, preferably monogrammed, the wording and spacing similar to those on the partially engraved invitations.

A prompt answer, in the same form in which they were issued, should be made to invitations received. A formal invitation in the third person should be answered in the third person, written by hand on personal stationery.

Sources of Information

Many times a secretary can improve her service by enlarging her knowledge of the subject covered in correspondence or reports. It is a comfort to remember that all man's knowledge is on record somewhere and available for reference—if only we know where to find it. By telephoning a specific question to the reference department of your city library you will obtain the information you need or else advice on how it may be found. But try to anticipate your problems by having good reference books in the office.

You ought to have a world atlas, by all means.

But the book you will consult most often will be the abridged dictionary that should be on your desk constantly. There are, of course, a number of good dictionaries, but the one recommended here is the most recent *Webster's New Collegiate Dictionary*, because it contains most of the information a secretary requires for her daily work: spelling, syllabication, pronunciation, meaning, usage, derivation, and even synonyms in many cases. You may value also the *Dictionary of American Synonyms* and *Roget's Thesaurus*, though in a busy office there is seldom time to consult these works.

Of course if it is possible for you to have the *World Almanac and Book of Facts* and an encyclopedia, that will give you considerable comfort when certain questions are posed. A copy of *Who's Who* will simplify your search for the initials and addresses of the important men and women with whom your employer corresponds. There is also a *Directory of Directors*, a *Directory of Merchants and Manufacturers*, and similar books, which appear annually. Ask the reference librarian at your city library to advise you which are best for your purpose.

If your employer has a literary turn of mind and is likely to insert a well-known quotation in his dictation now and then, you will be glad to have a copy of *Bartlett's Familiar Quotations*, to save him from misquoting.

Moody's Investment Service will provide information that your employer may need if he is a heavy investor in stocks and bonds. Your work will soon reveal whether you have use for the *List of Chambers of Commerce in the United States*, *Ayer's Directory of Newspapers and Periodicals*, or other specialized business compilations. *The Martindale-Hubbell Law Directory* is not often used outside of a law firm.

II

The Business Letter

Appearance

Scientific and constantly improving forms of communication are used all over the world, and the business letter ought not to be left in its obsolete form when it exerts such an enormous influence. It deserves close attention.

A concern is judged by its correspondence, as the stationery manufacturers so truthfully advertise. Very few customers ever see the home office or even any branch office, and receipt of an untidy or ungrammatical letter can give the impression that the service rendered by the company is equally negative. On the other hand, upon receiving a handsomely spaced and well-constructed letter, even without analyzing his own reaction, a customer is apt to believe it has emanated from an up-to-date office.

The skill of letter writing occupies one-third of office time, and it is the businessman's most effective advertisement as well as a lasting record. Most successful businessmen have already mastered the mechanics of language, but many who have risen to authoritative positions have had to neglect this particular refinement and are justified in relying on their secretaries to see that their letters are satisfactory. Thus, a secretary who has learned to speak correctly and who knows the proper way to use various parts of speech may still have to learn the technique of letter writing in order to win absentee friends for her employer.

The letter must of course be neat and without any typographical, grammatical, or spelling errors, and it must have a businesslike appearance that will not distract from the message it has to convey. The recipient must find it so appropriate that he thinks of nothing except what it says. This result can be obtained only by a letter neatly typed within symmetrical borders and by language that reaches straight to the heart of the matter discussed. It must also be within the convention of the commercial world, and that is the reason each company selects its own style for presentation to its public.

Paragraphing

It is not likely that the new secretary will be invited to decide on the style of letter used by the company, because, when she enters this office, a certain style is likely to have already been selected, after various experiments. She may be instructed to indent paragraphs or to block them, showing a double space between them when they are single-spaced. The employer will no doubt instruct her as to his way of closing the letter, perhaps with the company's name and his signature with title below. She will conform to his preference without question.

At the same time there will be mention of "open punctuation" (no marks at the end of each line outside the text of the letter) or "closed punctuation" (marks after the date line, after each line of the addressee's name and address, after the complimentary close, and after the signature). Usually, closed punctuation is used with indented paragraphs, while open punctuation is more often used with blocked paragraphs. The style must be consistent so that the company's correspondence will always be characteristic.

Beginning the Letter

Some offices show the "standard date line" near the body of the letter, ending at the right margin two spaces above the name of the addressee, which is written flush with the left margin. If the "centered date line" is chosen, it is placed two spaces below the letterhead as though it is a part of the letterhead—centered exactly, making the letter look well-balanced. If the company name and address in the letterhead fall in the center of the page, the centered date line can be effectively used. If the letterhead, however, is spread out across the whole top of the page, ending at the right margin, then the standard date line seems more graceful.

When paper without a letterhead is used, the date line must be standard and a part of the three-line heading. This consists of the address of the writer and the date of the letter:

> 1500 Northwest 79 Street
> Oklahoma City, Oklahoma
> May 27, 1968

Never place the name of the writer in the typewritten heading of the letter, for that belongs at the end of the letter.

In typing the date line, always use numerals for the day of the month (never adding *nd, d, rd, st,* or *th*), and never abbreviate the name of the month or use figures for it:

> Wrong: May 27th, 1967
> Right: May 27, 1967

If a street address is long enough to require two lines, place the less important of the two above:

> Student Union
> Northwestern State Teachers
>   College
> Alva, Oklahoma

If a company address is omitted on the letterhead, use a two-line address and the date at the top right of the page, as when writing on plain paper.

The name and address of the addressee should agree exactly with that typed on the envelope.

If an individual in a company is addressed, show the individual's name (and title) with the company's name below that, single-spaced. If there is a long address that must be carried over to a second line, indent the second line three spaces:

Mr. Charles F. Thomas, President
San Francisco National Bank and
    Mortgage Association
San Francisco, California

Never abbreviate part of the company name unless the company's registered name uses an abbreviation (e.g., Co., Inc., or &).

When you are writing to a person holding more than one office within a company, use the highest title, unless you are replying to a specific letter signed by him under another title, as applying to the subject covered. When you are writing to a department of a company, rather than to a person within the company, place the company name on the first line and the department on the second line.

Figures are used for all house numbers except One, and they are separated from a numerical street number by a dash:

3780—87 Street

The name of the city is never abbreviated, and in the best circles the names of states are always spelled out too.

Business titles are never abbreviated, and an individual's name is always preceded by *Mr., Mrs., Miss, Dr., Col.,* etc. It is permissible to place honorary initials after the name of an addressee, but in that case omit the beginning title:

Philip W. Radford, Ph.D.
not: Dr. Philip W. Radford, Ph.D.

Reverend and *Honorable* are titles of respect and are preceded by the word *The,* the *Mr.* being omitted.

In addressing women, *Miss* is used for an unmarried woman or for a divorcée who has resumed her maiden name; *Mrs.* with husband's full name for a married woman or a widow. If a divorcée retains her married name, use *Mrs.* plus her own name, not her husband's. Address a professional woman by her title, followed by her given and last names:

Dr. Mary Hungerford

When there is doubt as to the gender of the addressee, use *Mr.*

Never use an abbreviation for *Care of*; never use this term before a hotel name if the addressee is a guest there; never use it before a company name if the addressee is employed there. If he is temporarily receiving mail at the office of the company, *Care of* may be used before the company name:

> Mr. Joseph Mendelson
> Care of The Rockwell Company
> 60 Wall Street
> New York, N.Y.

An "attention line" refers the letter to the person or department in charge of the situation covered. The word *Attention* is followed by the name of the individual or department. Do not abbreviate the word *Attention* or follow it with a colon. The attention line is placed two spaces below the last line of the name and address of the addressee, flush with the left margin of the letter when paragraphs are blocked, or else in the center of the page when paragraphs are indented.

Of course the attention line is never used in a letter to an individual but only in a letter having a plural addressee, in which case the letter is written to the entire company and not to the person named in the attention line. Moreover, the salutation must always agree (singular or plural) with the name of the addressee, not with the name on the attention line.

The salutation is typed two spaces below the addressee's address or the attention line, flush with the left margin. The first word of the salutation begins with a capital, as does the name of the addressee:

> My dear Mrs. Thomas:
> Dear Governor Rockefeller:

In business letters the salutation is followed by a colon.

Sometimes you will be required to write a letter addressed to no particular person or firm (such as a letter of recommendation), and then you will use capitals for the salutation:

TO WHOM IT MAY CONCERN:

Many letters in business must begin with a subject line after the salutation. This is a valuable aid in the distribution of mail, and it also facilitates filing. The subject line can be centered, but, when the paragraphs are blocked, it is flush with the left margin.

Do not type *In re* or *Subject* before the subject line.

Underline the subject line, but, if it occupies more than one line, underline only the bottom line, letting the line extend to the length of the longest line in the subject.

Be sure to word the subject line so that it may be helpful. If the letter is about an order of silk, a subject line reading *Silk* would contribute nothing. If, however, the subject line should read, *Silk Returned, Our Shipping Order 8939,* the clerk opening the letter could promptly route it to the person within the organization best able to reply.

Contents

Now you have the body of the letter to consider, and you must judge how long the letter is and how much space it will occupy in order to place it on the page as within a frame. This will be difficult to judge when you are first taking a course in typing, but by the time you are a secretary you will have learned from experience just how to compose your page. You will accomplish this almost by a kinetic sense.

The material within the body of the letter must convey a message in straightforward language; further instruction in this matter is contained in the next chapter.

The letter should convey its message briefly, with the same ease that would be apparent in a personal interview. Even when a secretary must write whatever the employer dictates, many times while typing it she can ease the language somewhat to improve the impression upon the recipient, without calling her employer's attention to any change. It is her responsibility to see that the letter is creditable in every way to her employer's interests.

The length should be in accordance with the letter's importance. In addition, if it is too short, it may have a curt tone and thus may seem to slight the recipient; on the other hand, if it is too long, the recipient may wonder if the writer has nothing more to do with his time.

Closing the Letter

When the salutation has been *Dear Sir* or *My dear Sir,* the complimentary closing can be *Yours truly* or *Very truly yours,* when no personal connection exists between the writer and the recipient. *Sincerely yours* is appropriate where there is an established personal as well as business relationship, but it is used only in letters to individuals, never to a company. *Respectfully yours* appears only on letters addressed to a person of acknowledged authority.

Avoid the use of complimentary closes such as *Yours for lower prices* or *I remain* and other "hanging phrases." *Cordially yours* is not suitable in a business letter.

The signature on a business letter normally consists of the typed name of the company, a line for the writer's signature, and the typed name of the writer, with his title. It is typed in block form beginning under the first letter of the complimentary close. In some blocked-paragraph letters the complimentary close begins at the left margin; then the signature also begins at the left margin.

When, in the body of the letter, the writer has referred to *we, us,* or *our,* the company and not an individual in the company is writing the letter. Consequently, the company name is typed before the personal signature:

Very truly yours,
JONES BUILDING COMPANY

Philip W. Jones

Philip W. Jones, President

Never type a line for the writer's signature. This is superfluous and old-fashioned and serves no purpose.

When the writer has referred within the letter to *I, me, my,* or *mine,* this means that he, not the company, is writing the letter. Therefore the writer's name is typed with his title, omitting the company name:

Very truly yours,

Philip W. Jones

Philip W. Jones, President

An unmarried woman may sign as *(Miss) Louise A. Scott,* the *Miss* blocked with the complimentary close, not extended to the left of the signature. For a married woman the signature consists of the woman's first name and her surname, but under the signature there will be shown her husband's name preceded by *Mrs.*:

Sincerely yours,

Mary Bryan

Mrs. John R. Bryan

A widow signs as though her husband were living. A divorced woman no longer uses the given name or initial of her former husband. If she has not reverted to her maiden name and taken the title *Miss,* then her signature becomes her first name, the initial of her maiden name, and her married surname:

Sincerely yours,

Genevieve Y. Brown

Mrs. Genevieve Y. Brown

It is no longer considered good form to type the initials of the dictator, a colon, and then the typist's initials; if the company requires identification of this kind for their files, however, show these on the file copy only, not on the original. To save the trouble of reinserting the file copy in the typewriter, slip a small memo sheet between the platen and the ribbon as a guard when you type the initials flush with the left margin, two spaces lower on the page than the signature.

It serves no purpose to add *enc 2* if the body of the letter mentions the enclosure of two papers. But, should the mailing department find this helpful to them, then place it directly beneath the identification initials if any are used.

Sometimes the dictator will take advantage of a postscript

(following the initials *P.S.* two spaces below the last line) to dramatize some bit of information. But never make the mistake of adding in a postscript something forgotten during the typing of the letter. It is far better to take the time to retype the entire letter.

Before you consider the letter finished, survey it to decide if it looks like a picture on the page; that is, have you centered the whole thing? Check carefully your grammar, spelling, and punctuation.

If *you* should receive this letter, would *you* be favorably impressed with the company from which it came?

The folding of a business letter must be precise, neat, and efficient in economizing human energy, especially when large numbers of letters are involved. The side edges must match, the typing inside the fold must seem to be protected, and only the fewest folds necessary for perfect fit into the envelope must be used.

The unfolding should be considered. Upon taking the letter from the envelope the recipient should be able to begin reading the letter immediately, and he should find it attractive. Remember, this may be his first impression of your organization.

III

Secretarial Duties

Opening the Mail

Many an employer is willing to let his secretary select from the incoming mail the letters that she herself can answer over her own signature or his, depending upon the importance of the matter. The secretary's judgment should be guided by her experience and her knowledge of the subject covered.

Go to the trouble of ordering a rubber date stamp so that you can stamp each piece of incoming mail as it is opened. This can be done as a matter of habit, and then, in the one time out of a hundred when it is important to your employer to know exactly when a certain letter or document reached the office, you will have the record. At night turn your ink pad upside down to let the ink flow to the top and be fresh for your use the next morning.

When opening the morning mail the secretary should first consider the telegrams, the special deliveries, the airmail, and then the remainder of the first-class mail. When opening envelopes check for possible enclosures and attach them to the covering letter. Be sure also that the name and address of the writer and the date of his writing are on the letter before you discard the envelope. You will notice that often some of the letters will cause your employer to ask for the pertinent file; if you can anticipate his request you will be saving his time and yours.

Letters Written by the Secretary

These will usually include acknowledgment of correspondence received while the employer is absent; letters requesting appointments; reservation letters (for hotel, plane, and train); follow-up letters; and letters requesting information that another secretary can furnish. But the secretary should always keep in mind that service to her employer is the main factor in her deciding which letters to write without dictation.

Planning the Letter

Good ideas can be clouded by verbosity, while forceful and clear words assure the recipient's quick understanding. Therefore plan the letter before you write a word. The time element is the greatest cost connected with a letter, and one well-planned will insure a minimum of reorganization.

Ask yourself: Is the letter supposed to serve the writer, the recipient, or both? What data must the letter contain? Will it give information or will it request information? Be sure that the full file on the subject is on your desk so that you can readily refer to previous correspondence or grasp the information to be relayed before you begin to write. Of course if the writer is hazy about the subject or the product mentioned, he cannot expect the recipient to get a clear picture from his words.

In the first sentence mention the purpose of the letter so as to alert the recipient, then follow with whatever explanation is necessary, using a positive tone at all times—in words chosen to evoke a positive result. Speak directly to the recipient from his own viewpoint, not merely from yours. The recipient must see that it is to his advantage to reply favorably.

Use concise language, but be as natural as possible, as though your words were being spoken. Reserve the last sentence to request a response if there is to be further correspondence on this subject, and always make that last sentence complete. Avoid a hanging statement such as "Hoping this meets with your approval, I am . . ." If that is the thought you wish to express, state it this way: "I hope this meets with your approval."

In a business letter there is no place for clever remarks or badinage, and it is wise never to use slang. Resorting to slang, after all, may be construed as a confession that you do not know the correct English equivalent. Besides, slang becomes outdated rapidly. Avoid also any sign of exaggeration, sarcasm, or remarks derogatory to anyone or any product.

By relying on your integrity in handling the subject, you will automatically produce a logical and appropriate letter.

For the Employer's Signature

The employer may prefer that all letters be written over his name rather than some being written over his secretary's, even though she composes the replies and writes his signature. In signing his name, she ought to duplicate his handwriting as nearly as possible or at least make a firm and interesting signature of it.

When the secretary writes a letter in her employer's behalf but in her own name, she signs it but does not type her name below the signature:

Sincerely yours,

Mae Johnson

Secretary to Mr. Wilson

not: Sincerely yours,

Mae Johnson

(Miss) Mae Johnson
Secretary to Mr. R. E. Wilson

Avoid the discourtesy of writing "Dictated but not read" or "Signed in Mr. Wilson's absence." It hints at disloyalty to the secretary, by the way, as though she could not be trusted to write what the employer asked her to write.

Neither should the secretary sign her employer's name and attach her initials beside it. If you find it useful to record the true writer and signer, make a notation on the file copy only.

Write the letter as if your employer were speaking to the person addressed, using his characteristic language. If he dictates in a short, concise manner, word this letter the same way. If he usually goes into detail, do the same. In other words, make the reader think that your employer dictated the letter and signed it. Thus, you can consider yourself a "ghost-writer," for this is the same method used by many who prepare books to appear under the names of famous men and women.

Routine Letters

If you notice that your employer frequently dictates a routine letter, encourage him to trust you with this branch of the work to save his time. When he finds out that you can prepare such letters for his signature without dictation, he will feel gratified.

Acknowledgments

The secretary should acknowledge letters received during her employer's absence and may also give the information requested if she knows it. Otherwise, she may indicate that the letter has been received and will be called to her employer's attention immediately upon his return.

Appointments

The secretary may request an appointment for her employer, or she may reply to letters requesting an appointment with him. In each such letter she should always refer to the reason for the appointment and the suggested time, requesting a confirmation.

If a certain time has been requested and your employer approves, fix the appointment accordingly. If he will be otherwise occupied at the requested time, suggest another and ask for confirmation. Be sure to keep a record of the appointments suggested and not yet confirmed. If there is ever an argument that your employer broke an appointment you will be able to exonerate him.

Reservations

In writing for hotel reservations, state the type of accommodation desired, the name of the person desiring it, and the date and time of arrival, with probable date of departure. Then request confirmation.

No doubt the usual reservations for plane and train travel will be made through a travel agent who understands your employer's requirements and will make every effort to satisfy. If so, a telephone call should be substituted for a letter.

Follow-Up

In some offices the follow-up file is known as the tickler file, and that shows an amusing view of the way the secretary must check on delayed replies after a certain lapse of time. In her follow-up letter she should refer to the previous correspondence, identifying the last letter by date as well as content, and perhaps enclosing a copy of it if it contains a great deal of detail that could be useful should the original letter be unavailable to the addressee.

If you have many follow-up letters to write, instead of composing separate reminders, prepare a form request that can be run off on the duplicator. Often the enclosure of a stamped return envelope will convey to your correspondent the idea that you are in a hurry for a reply.

Congratulations and Condolence

There are times when a businessman must write a personal letter to other businessmen. The secretary is often instructed to write such a letter to be signed by the employer's name, and it must display sincerity.

When congratulations or condolences are to be extended to a business acquaintance, or when thanks for similar messages must be sent, the secretary will use the salutation that she knows her employer would normally use and will sign the name that he is called by the recipient.

Dear John:

I have just read in the *Wall Street Journal* of your promotion to General Sales Manager. I don't think that Smith and Company could have chosen a better man for the job. My congratulations to you.

Sincerely yours,

Phil

Dear John:

I appreciate your generous letter about my promotion to Executive Vice President. Such good wishes and kind words will help me do a better job, I am sure.

Thanks for your note and for your valued friendship.

Sincerely yours,

Phil

Dear Mrs. Wilson:

It is with great regret that I just read of your son's death.

I know there are no words of mine that can console you in this sorrowful time, but I do want you to know of my deepest sympathy. You have many friends who are thinking of you.

Sincerely yours,

Philip Brown

Philip Brown, President

Dear Mr. Crenshaw:

All of us at Thorne and Sons were saddened to learn of your wife's death. We know there is nothing we can say to help you in this time of grief, but we do want you to know that we extend to you our very deep sympathy.

Sincerely yours,

Philip Brown

Philip Brown

Dear Mr. Holmes:

We at Liberty Oil Company are sorry to read of the tornado that struck your factory. We know the loss was great, but we know also that you will rise and go ahead with rebuilding.

If we can be of service in helping you overcome your present problems, please call on us. We have enjoyed doing business with R. G. Holmes Company and look forward to resuming our relationship in the near future.

Sincerely yours,

Philip Brown

Philip Brown, President

Dear Henry:

Your card and beautiful bouquet helped a great deal to make last week bearable to me.

I am back at the office and feel I shall be as good as ever before many days have passed. The accident was a shock, but with good friends like you I know the days ahead will be brighter.

You may be sure that I appreciate your friendship all the more at a time like this.

Sincerely yours,

Phil

Personal Service and Hospitality

When a person has done your employer a personal service or has entertained him when he is out of town without financial remuneration, he should be thanked in a letter that can be written by the secretary:

Dear Joe:

If it hadn't been for your keen mind and able assistance our recent sales meeting might have been a complete flop. Because I had never before conducted such a meeting, I certainly was lucky to have your help.

Thanks for your good judgment and wise suggestions.

Sincerely yours,

Phil

Introductions

Letters of introduction written by the secretary for her employer's signature may be either mailed or prepared for delivery in person. Such letters should of course contain the name of the introduced person, the reason for the introduction, the personal or business qualifications of the person, and a courtesy statement.

To a business associate:

Dear Mr. Fielding:

This will introduce a good friend of mine, John August, who is associated with our State De-

partment of Commerce. He has heard of the
fine work you are doing in Ohio and hopes he
will have a chance to talk with you for a few
minutes when he visits your city next Tuesday,
March 22.

I have asked Mr. August to telephone you upon
his arrival in Cincinnati, to learn whether you
can see him on that day. If you can, I shall
appreciate it. I think you will enjoy meeting
him.

It was fine to see you at the Dallas convention,
and I look forward to the Los Angeles convention in September.

Sincerely yours,

Philip Brown

Philip Brown, President

To a personal friend:

Dear Tom:

A very good friend of mine, John August, will
be passing through Memphis on his way to
New York next Tuesday, and I have asked him
to stop by your office. John is a fellow you will
enjoy meeting.

I shall, of course, appreciate any courtesy you
may extend to him while he is in Memphis—
his first visit to your city, by the way.

Sincerely yours,

Phil

Invitation

Letters of invitation should be gracious without undue
formality. Always tell *when* and *where* and *why*, if the occasion justifies it.

To attend a luncheon or dinner:

Dear Mr. Blake:

The American Service Life Insurance Company is holding a dinner next Thursday evening honoring their million-dollar-a-year men. Will you join us as our honored guest?

Since you would be seated at the head table, we are asking you to join us in Room 9 of the Waldorf Hotel at seven thirty, so that we may arrive at the banquet room in a group.

Sincerely yours,

Norman Drake

Norman Drake, President

Dear Roger:

Arthur Whitfield is coming to town next Friday, and Bill Terrell and I are entertaining him at a luncheon at the Ritz. We hope you can set aside a couple of hours so as to join us. I am sure Arthur will be happy to see you, as Bill and I shall also.

The luncheon will be held in the Persian Room at twelve fifteen.

Sincerely yours,

Paul

To give an address:

Dear Mr. Lee:

As President of the Chicago Rotary Club, I have been asked to arrange the program for our next Thursday noon meeting. I know that all of our Chicago Rotarians would like to hear the address you gave in Detroit last week (I was privileged to be in attendance there) on the subject of "The International Situation."

Next Thursday's meeting will be held in the Venetian Room of the Drake Hotel. I hope you will be with us to give our members the same treat you afforded the Detroit Rotarians.

Sincerely yours,

Philip Brown

Philip Brown, President

Accepting an invitation to give an address:

Dear Mr. Brown:

I shall be delighted to speak to the Chicago Rotary Club next Thursday. Thank you for inviting me.

Your suggestion that I repeat my Detroit address means that I won't have to prepare a new one.

I shall look forward to seeing you in the Venetian Room at noon.

Sincerely yours,

Barrymore Lee

Barrymore Lee

Declination

Letters declining an invitation should express appreciation and enthusiasm with assurance of regret or an explanation.

Dear Mr. Brett:

Only yesterday I accepted an invitation to speak in Boston on July 4, the date of your dinner meeting honoring your million-dollar-a-year men. This will make it impossible for me to be your guest that evening.

It was kind of you to invite me, and I regret my inability to attend. I hope the occasion will be a very successful one.

Sincerely yours,

Arthur D. Haas

Arthur D. Haas

My dear Mrs. Scott:

In reply to your letter of May 3 inviting me to participate in your association's fund-raising campaign, I appreciate your thoughtfulness in writing me.

I am familiar with your association's good work, and in the past it has been my pleasure to contribute to it. It is with regret, therefore, that I must tell you that all my available funds for purposes of this nature have been pledged. It is just not possible for me to be a party of your worthy program at this time.

You have my best wishes for a highly successful campaign.

Sincerely yours,

Philip Brown

Philip Brown, President

Canceling a speaking engagement:

Dear Mr. Bryson:

I dislike writing a letter that will cause someone inconvenience, but this one falls within that category, to my sorrow.

This morning, I was advised that a close relative had passed away in Denver, and I shall be leaving this afternoon to attend the funeral tomorrow, the day of your meeting.

I regret that I shall not be able to speak to your group and especially that you will have to find a speaker to replace me at this late date. I hope that you will understand that I am helpless to avoid this trip.

I hope your meeting will be successful in every way.

Sincerely yours,

Philip Brown

Philip Brown, President

(The preceding letter would be delivered by messenger immediately or would be telegraphed if the addressee is in another city.)

Acceptance

Letters of acceptance should be brief, appreciative, and enthusiastic. If the letter of invitation failed to include complete details, the letter of acceptance should ask for specific information.

Dear Mr. Brett:

It is a pleasure to accept your invitation to attend the dinner next Thursday evening honoring your million-dollar-a-year men.

I shall be in Room 9 of the Waldorf Hotel promptly at seven-thirty, as you suggest.

Thank you very much for your invitation.

Sincerely yours,

Philip Brown

Philip Brown

Model Letters

For letters that are typical of situations that arise frequently, make an extra copy to keep in a special binder so that you can refer to it and use it as a model when you have reason to write that sort of letter again. On the copy of each such letter note the space plan for margins and center measurements, so that you will have the format already arranged.

Interoffice Memoranda

Memoranda should be written on plain paper unless special company forms are provided. They should be directed only to persons within the organization and not to outsiders and should be signed or initialed by the dictator. If a memorandum is confidential in nature, it should be enclosed in a sealed envelope. If copies are sent to others than the person addressed, notation to that effect should be made at the lower left corner of the form.

Postcards

In communicating advertising material to customers or making special offers, double postcards can save time. It is thus easy for the customer to reply promptly by merely tearing off his side of the card and jotting down the simple answers on printed blanks.

Mailing List

If you have a mailing list in which the addresses of your regular customers are likely to change frequently, use a card index in a card-file box with alphabetical guides. The changes can be made by replacement or removal of cards, and in this way you can keep your mailing list up to date. Otherwise you

may find too large a percentage of your outgoing mail is
returned marked *Unknown*.

Preparation for a Meeting

Every corporation holds an annual meeting of stockholders
for the election of directors. During the year it may hold
other meetings when stockholders' consent is required for
some proposed action, such as an increase or decrease in
capital stock, an amendment of the corporate charter, or a
merger.

The secretary will usually have to prepare notices of the
meeting, together with a proxy form to be used in case a
stockholder cannot attend. This proxy gives another person
the right to vote for the stockholder. These must be sent to
everyone concerned, in accordance with the bylaws of the
group that is meeting.

The secretary must confirm that the meeting place has
been engaged and will be ready for use at the time specified.
She will usually type the agenda and place all pertinent
papers in a folder with the corporate seal on the conference
table at the chairman's seat.

If the secretary acts as the recorder of the meeting, she is
seated beside the chairman in order to hear every word
distinctly. If she cannot hear, she signals the chairman, who
then asks for a repetition of what has been said. Before the
meeting, she should know its purpose and should have read
all resolutions and reports to be presented. She should also
have a list of the persons attending and check the absentees
ahead of time rather than write down names while the roll is
being called. The greater her knowledge of the meeting, the
more easily she will do the recording.

Minutes

The secretary's transcription of the minutes should be in
formal language according to the following outline:

1. Name of organization
2. Name of body conducting meeting
3. Date and hour and location of meeting
4. List of those present and those absent
5. Reading of previous minutes and their approval or
   emendation

  6. Unfinished business
  7. New business
  8. Date of next meeting
  9. Time of adjournment
 10. Signature of recorder.

Following is a report of a typical meeting:

MINUTES
of Meeting of
the Historical Society of the University of Oklahoma
Lockett Hotel, Norman, Oklahoma
May 1, 1966

At the meeting of the Historical Society of the University of Oklahoma, some 100 charter members being present, the Society was called to order at 1:05 p.m. by Mr. John R. Combs, Chairman, who requested Mr. William T. Scaggs to serve as Temporary Secretary.

Mr. Combs dispensed with the reading of the Minutes of the last meeting because a copy had been previously distributed to all members.

A communication from the National Historical Society, read and accepted by the Society, dealt with the planting of redbud trees throughout America.

A communication from Mr. Harvey Allen of New York City, New York, asked that the Society refrain from their normal pattern of conducting Spring Tours throughout the State of Oklahoma. Several members, after the reading, expressed disagreement with the views given by Mr. Allen.

There was no unfinished business.

New business was the election of officers for the remaining current year. The following nominations were announced by Mr. William T. Scaggs, Chairman of the Nominating Committee:

President	Mrs. Rutherford R. Tinsdale
Secretary	Miss Alene Mapes
Treasurer	Mrs. Theodore R. Tolliver
Members of	Miss Louise Allen
the Council	Mrs. Philip W. Crossman
	Mrs. John Stobaugh
	Mrs. John C. McCann

After an unanswered call for nominations from the floor, it was moved by Mrs. William R. Metcalfe that the Secretary cast one ballot for officers nominated. The motion was seconded and carried, and the officers were declared elected.

After congratulations to the newly elected officers by the Chairman, the Society adjourned at 3:25 P.M.

William T. Scaggs

William T. Scaggs
Temporary Secretary

Resolutions

Formal resolutions may be made in one of these forms:

> WHEREAS it is necessary to . . . . ; and
> WHEREAS conditions are such that . . . ; and
> WHEREAS, moreover, on the 5th day of August, 1960,
> . . . . ; Therefore be it
> RESOLVED, That . . . ; and be it
> RESOLVED further, That . . .

Note that the word WHEREAS is in caps with no comma following it; the first word after it is not capitalized unless it is a proper name. The word RESOLVED is also set in caps but is followed by a comma and a capital letter.

In informal resolutions the facts are stated simply:

> . . . and the following resolution was unanimously adopted:
> RESOLVED, That . . .

Conference Notes

If your employer should ask you to report on all that is said in a conference, make place cards for the members of the group expected to meet. As they enter the room, direct them to sit where they have been assigned. Then you can be sure, according to the direction from which each remark emanates around the conference table, whose voice you are recording.

Before your own seat, arrange tabs showing the names of the members in the same order as they are seated around the table. You will immediately know whose voice is contributing to the discussion at each given moment. This will enable you to take your notes in the form of a dramatic dialogue: Preface one remark with *Hansen* if the man whose name is Hansen has spoken, then preface the next remark with *Rosen* if the next voice has come from the seat you assigned to Mr. Rosen.

When you transcribe your notes, you can show the discussion in this dialogue form, if that is acceptable to your employer; or, you can insert a full "stage direction," such as "Mr. Hansen replied:" or "The next speaker was Mr. Rosen, who said:". You will probably find that your employer is pleased with your plan to show the names to the left of the remarks quoted. In any case, you should open your transcription with a list of those present, giving full name or initials and office held, if any, for each.

Stenotyping is used for the recording of many conferences as well as for court trials; when there is only an occasional necessity for such recording, however, the trained secretary can do quite as well with her shorthand. One advantage of stenotyping is that the notes can be transcribed by anyone at all who has taken the course in stenotyping, even after the lapse of some time.

These days a recording device is frequently available, but the secretary should be ready if it is not. It may be wise for the secretary to take her own notes in some cases, if she is expected to decipher the recording, because unless the meeting is held under strict discipline there may be a jumble of voices. At such times personal attendance can enhance the use of the recorder.

IV

Typing

Efficiency Tips

When starting to type a letter, insert the paper in the carriage of the typewriter so that its left edge is at "0" on the machine's scale. Determine on the scale the exact center of a single line to be typed and set your margins in such a way that the line (no matter what its length) will be in the center of the page.

Plan to use single spacing unless the letter is to be less than fifty words in length. Then it is natural to double-space, though the addressee's name and address will be single-spaced as always.

When you prefer not to double-space for a short letter, set the margins so that each line will be four or five inches long instead of the usual six inches. Half the length to be used, subtracted from the number at the center, gives you the left margin set. The same amount of length following the center number will show the point at which the typewriter bell should be set to ring.

When you are transcribing notes, stand your notebook up on its tentlike covers, for it is easier to read the shorthand rapidly when the page is vertical than when it is horizontal.

Have your stationery drawer organized with slanting compartments to hold the various kinds of paper so that you can almost automatically draw out a letterhead or a sheet for the carbon copy. Have the envelopes of various sizes also in such position that your hand can easily select the one you need.

If the body of the letter is long enough to occupy more than one page (with adequate space at bottom of the first page to match the side margins), there must be at least two lines of the letter to carry over to the second page before the complimentary close. Second and succeeding pages are typed on matching plain paper, never on letterhead paper. These extra pages start with a typed heading six lines from the top edge of the paper. This heading, written on one line, starts at the left margin with the addressee's name; the page number is placed in the center with no parentheses or period or dash; and the date ends at the right margin. To end the date at the right margin, place the type bar guide at the right margin, backspace the number of characters contained in the date, then begin typing the date.

If you find it necessary to type a name beneath a signature after the paper has been removed from the typewriter, especially after the paper has been stapled to others, use a blank sheet in the carriage, back it down on the roll of the platen until only its top inch is visible, then let the bottom of your typed sheet lower into the carriage behind the top of that blank sheet rolled down below the ribbon contact. At the proper place you can type the name (or other last line) on the page that was finished earlier.

If you can obtain micrometric carbon paper (with the white tab running along the right edge of the whole sheet, showing line numbers) you will be able to comfortably end the typing of each page at the same distance from the bottom by observing the line number. On long letters, as well as on reports and tabulations and legal documents, you will find this of great assistance in keeping a consistent lower margin on all papers.

There are also backing sheets for this purpose, to be used behind the last carbon copy next to the platen. The right-hand marginal numbers are a convenience.

Erasures

Never use an eraser where its broken particles may fall into the mechanical parts of the typewriter. By pressing the margin release you can move the carriage to right or left and thus erase where the fragments can fall to the desk instead of between the key bars to be caked together, thus jeopardizing your speed and damaging the machine.

A curved steel erasure guard that can hug the curve of the platen, when placed between the original copy and the carbon sheet behind it, will protect the carbon copies while you erase an error. A soft eraser can then be used in preparing the carbon copies for the correction to be typed. To be sure that you do not erase more than the one or two letters that need to be changed, use a cellophane shield with open slots of the size of one letter, two letters, or a series in case a whole word has to be erased.

There are on the market patented sheets caked with white designed to cancel any "typo" you may have made. These are useful for offset printing (where the black and white contrast is the main consideration). But for letters and manuscripts and legal documents that must make a neat (and lasting) appearance the good old erasure cannot be surpassed.

Of course where you want only perfection you will retype any page that has shown an error.

Care of the Typewriter

Always be sure to cover your typewriter before you leave the office so that dust will not impair its usefulness. If you are using an electric typewriter make a habit of turning off the current at the same time. Although the secretary will take pride in keeping her machine clean, the office manager will probably arrange an annual maintenance contract; then a monthly inspection will guarantee the good condition of the machine, saving the secretary the necessity of oiling the parts.

But clean the type periodically and change the ribbon often enough to give every page you type a fresh look.

The secretary's skill in typing in rhythm will ensure a longer life for the machine, and she should insist on having a firm desk which cannot be shaken to cause friction within the delicate mechanism. If she has a chair high enough to enable her hands to work while the elbows are as low as her waist, she will show speed without ever tiring.

Headings

A heading always stands alone on a line with no period or dash following it.

Main headings are centered and in caps, not underlined. The letters may be spaced out for added effect. Subheadings are centered and underlined, with main words begun in capitals. Side headings are typed at the left margin and underlined, with main words begun in capitals.

MAIN HEADING   (all caps, spaced)

Subheading   (centered, underlined)

Side heading   (flush with left margin, underlined)

Headings are underlined without a break between words. On headings longer than one line, the last line only is underlined. If the last line is shorter than a previous line, extend the underlining to the length of the longest line in that heading.

If a heading occupies more than one line, it is divided only at a logical pause:

Boats, Tackle, and Bait
Supplied by Owner

In numbered headings, Roman numerals are used for the main subject; capital letters are used for numbering the secondary subject; Arabic numerals for tertiary subjects; and small letters for lesser subjects. No period is given after Roman numerals, only after Arabic numerals or alphabetical letters. Parentheses are not used.

Following is an example of numbered headings:

I   International Cooperation
   A.   Various Nations
      1.   Officials in Agreement
         a.   Steps Taken
   B.   Resolutions Rejected
      1.   Officials Declining
         a.   Reasons Given
         b.   Remedies Suggested

2. Debate Scheduled
    a. Time and Place
    b. Agenda
II Activities Recommended . . .

Tabulation

Aside from use in setting left and right margins and paragraph indentations, the tabulator is of value in the placement of the complimentary close and signature line in letters and also in preparing the position of columns in tables. A table usually has three parts: title, columnar headings, and side headings. Words are aligned on the left, figures on the right. Headings are centered.

Use a three-line space between title and subheading, if any, or between the title and columnar headings, if any. Use a two-line space between the subheading and the columnar headings, and a two-line space between the columnar headings and the items in the column. Use a double space in the list if the table is short, otherwise a single space.

To center a heading, count the letters, spaces, and punctuation marks in it and divide this number by two. Subtract that number from the center number on your typewriter scale. If the center point is 41 on the carriage scale, and the heading to be centered is BROWN, SMITH, THOMPSON & WILLIAMS, which occupies 33 spaces, your left margin for that heading would be 41 minus 17 (half of 33), or 24 on the carriage scale.

Stationery

The selection of a company's letterhead is a matter of pride and should not be made in a haphazard manner. The employer may consult with his secretary as to her preference if he decides to start using a new design.

The standard size of the business sheet on which the letterhead appears is 8½" x 11". Most files, envelopes, and business machines are geared to the use of this size. Although 20-pound paper is acceptable, the best paper for letters is sold as 24-pound. Paper weight is measured by the ream, five hundred sheets. Substance 24-pound letterhead paper implies that two thousand sheets of this size will weigh twenty-four pounds.

Today's business is concerned mainly with the selling of goods and services at a profit, and, if a customer receives a carelessly written letter on poor-quality paper, he may conclude that the organization is not reliable. But the same person, upon receiving from the same organization a well-planned, consistently typed letter on high-grade paper with an equally impressive letterhead, either printed or engraved, will decide that the company is one he can deal with profitably.

The grade and shade of the paper should "blend" with the type of organization using it. The same shade (though not necessarily the same quality) may be used throughout the organization for invoices, purchase orders, statements, and other forms.

Many conservative business firms use nothing but white paper with a black letterhead. Other businesses, however, select colors appropriate to their up-to-date ideas. A shop specializing in infant wear could use light-blue stationery with a darker letterhead; a tree nursery could use green; a novelty shop should use stationery chosen particularly to attract the eye.

It is important to realize, though, that the letterhead ought never to distract from the purpose of the letter typed upon it, which is to convey a message.

Envelopes should be of the same quality and color as the sheets. If the letterhead is engraved, the return address on the envelope should also be engraved. Window envelopes are used only for sending statements, checks, or advertising announcements.

V

Filing

Many companies have a central file where papers from all departments within the organization are kept by competent clerks. But every secretary will have an executive's file to maintain in her own office: confidential letters, personal documents, annual and quarterly reports from companies whose stock her employer holds, progress statements on cash or margin accounts held with his broker, and records of his securities and other investments. She must be able to find any of these at a moment's notice.

Before starting to do the day's filing, prepare your papers by separating the personal correspondence from the business correspondence and documents. Check all papers that are stapled to be sure that only papers belonging together have been stapled together. Remove all paper clips, because they not only crowd the file but also sometimes catch papers that ought not to be clipped to them, causing an unfortunate loss of those papers that cannot be found under their own title. Mend any torn papers with Scotch tape. Underline in red pencil the name or subject under which the paper is to be filed.

On the file folders, staggered tabs or one-position tabs may be used. The straight-line tab, all in the center or in the far right position on the edge of the folder, are often preferred.

When various sets of files are used, it is wise to tab each set with a different color label: white for correspondence, blue for subject, green for case.

On gummed labels type the name of the folder on the first line below the folding line, beginning two or three spaces from the left edge; use initial caps and small letters and abbreviate freely; leave two spaces between name and any number.

Filing Systems

Alphabetical

If the office is small, the most efficient method is to arrange the material alphabetically according to name. No cross-indexing is necessary. A gummed label should be typed for each name and attached to the tab on the folder. Papers are placed in the folder in chronological order with the latest date in front. The folders are filed behind alphabet guides.

When there is voluminous correspondence with one customer, several folders will be required to hold all the current material, and then it is a good practice to separate the material into time periods: one folder for the year 1965, another for 1966, another for 1967. Or if several projects have been conducted for that customer, one folder may be labeled *Florida*, another *North Dakota*, another *Michigan*, and so on.

Geographical

Where the geographical location is the deciding factor, material is classified by the name of the place, with subordinate folders labeled with the names of correspondents in each place. Standard geographical guide sets are obtainable from office supply stores. A disadvantage of this system is that it, like the numerical system, requires a cross-index with cards filed alphabetically. A paper must therefore be found either by checking the name of the place or the name of the correspondent.

Numerical

Material arranged by numbers is used only in scientific

work, with a cross-index that shows what each number represents on cards arranged alphabetically by subject or name. This system has the advantage of being accurate and may be rapidly consulted. The disadvantage is the maintenance of the card index and the occasional need for a second search when a paper is wanted.

Decimal

Used principally in libraries, this system is based on the Dewey decimal classification system. The material must be organized under ten or fewer main headings, numbered 000 to 900. In turn, each main heading is divided into ten or fewer subheadings, numbered from 10 to 90, preceded by the correct hundreds digit. Each subheading may then be subdivided into ten or fewer further headings numbered from 1 to 9, preceded by the correct hundreds and tens digits.

Soundex

This "group-name system" is used when there are a great many names involved, as in census surveys. Names that sound alike but are spelled differently—such as Nielsen, Neilson, and Nealson—are grouped together according to pronunciation rather than spelling.

Subject

This classification is used when papers are called for by subject rather than by a person's name. The secretary should be thoroughly familiar with the material that flows through her office before attempting to set up this kind of file. The list of subjects must be comprehensive and as simple as possible, in alphabetical order or by number code. The alphabetical is usually preferred, because then a cross-index is not necessary. Papers in the subject folder are arranged chronologically, the latest date in front.

Subject Index

While an index is not required for a small filing system, it is imperative for large companies. The index will prevent the filing of material under a new heading when a folder has already been set up for that subject under a different title, and it permits a person other than the secretary to trace things in the file.

A card is made for each subject heading or subheading. Each subheading shows the main heading under which it is filed. Cross-reference cards are made if the subject is complex. The employer may indicate on the paper where he wants it to be filed, while the secretary may have formerly filed that subject under another heading. A cross-reference enables both to find the paper later. The index cards are filed alphabetically.

Out Cards

To maintain control of material borrowed from the file, guides of the same height as the file folders but of differently colored stock are used. The word *OUT* is printed on the tab. On this *OUT* card, space is provided for the date and designation of the material, the date it was removed from the file, the date it is to be returned, the person removing it, and for a remarks column.

Follow-Up File

Correspondence needing attention later is written with an extra carbon copy that is placed in the tickler file for reference at a specified date. Original papers are never placed in a follow-up file.

The tabs on the folders in this file are labeled with numbers from 1 to 31, so that the secretary can consult them each day of the month as indicated. The papers that need not be handled until the following month are left until the right date occurs in the next month.

On the proper day the secretary writes a follow-up letter or calls the matter to her employer's attention for his action.

Chronological Desk File

When correspondence is voluminous, it is a good idea to keep a carbon copy of each letter in a binder on the desk or near at hand, so that a recent letter may be referred to quickly without requiring a trip to the regular file.

Transfer

When there is obviously too much material crammed into a file cabinet, the secretary should take the time to prepare a transfer file—keeping out-of-date material in properly labeled folders and with the date clear on the tabs. These folders can be filed as usual, but in an overflow cabinet in a less conspicuous part of the office, considering that it will be consulted more seldom than the recent correspondence.

Alphabetizing for Indexing

If the first and second words to be indexed are the same, the position is naturally determined by the letters that follow:

> Smith, Mary B.
> Smith, Ned
> Smithson, John.

When two or more similar names are of unequal length, file the shorter name first:

> National Bank
> National Bank of Commerce
>
> Smith, M.
> Smith, Mary
> Smith, Mary C.
> Smith, Mary Charlene.

Words joined by a hyphen are treated as one word. However, in a firm name, if the hyphen is used instead of a comma, the individual parts of the name are treated as separate words:

> Down-Town Drug Company
> Johnson-Smith & Co.

If a firm name is composed of a compound word spelled as a

single word or spelled as two words, it is indexed as the word is written but considered as one word when alphabetizing:

> Newdeal Loan Co.
> New Deal Loan Company
> Newdeal Marine Works
> Southeast Shipbuilding Co.
> South East Tannery.

Single letters used as words are treated as words and arranged alphabetically, preceding word-names:

> BB Shop
> BBB Service Co.
> Betty Sue Shop
> Brighton Clothes Co.

Abbreviations are alphabetized as if spelled in full:

Name	*Filed as*
James Smith	Smith, James
Jas. Smith	Smith, James
St. Luke's Church	Saint Luke's Church
Chas. Williams	Williams, Charles.

Designations following names are alphabetized according to natural order of age:

> Smith, James, 2nd
> Smith, James III
> Smith, James, Jr.
> Smith, James, Sr.

Articles, prepositions, conjunctions, and the ampersand are disregarded in alphabetizing:

> Thomas & Anderson, Inc.
> Thomas, Browning R.
> Washington Bank, The
> Workshop for the Blind.

Individual surnames compounded with prefixes are indexed as written but in alphabetizing are treated as one word, the apostrophe, space, and capitalization (if any) being disregarded:

> Danders, John
> D'Andrea, R. A.

D'Andrea, Robert C.
De Jong, C. A.
De La Tare, M. A.

If a name contains a number, alphabetize it as if the number were spelled out:

13 Park Avenue
3029 Building Corp (three thousand twenty-nine).
21 Club.

Titles are disregarded:

Jones, R. L. (Dr.)
Simms, Carlotta (Countess)
Smith, Nancy (Miss).

Exception: If a firm name starts with a title, the title is considered to be the first word:

Queen Mary Boat Co.
Sir John Thomas Cigar Company
Viceroy of India Silk Co.

VI

Communication Services

Telephone

Manners

The secretary must have a pleasing telephone personality and a well-modulated voice that shows dignity as well as courtesy. Because she is not seen by the person at the other end of the line (though visual telephoning is becoming more available daily), she is judged, and her employer is judged, by the friendliness of her telephone voice. She must always show interest in what is being said to her, and she must reply in clear tones, never raising her voice.

For the sake of out-of-town visitors who may phone you to ask the route to your part of the city, it is good to have a map of the locality on the wall near the telephone. You can then show the extra courtesy of plotting their trip from the airport, the railroad station, or a freeway.

When the phone rings, answer it as soon as possible. If you must leave your desk, ask someone to answer your phone for you during your absence and explain where you can be located.

Always have a memo pad near the phone; never be guilty of having to say, "Wait until I find a pencil." If it is necessary for you to delay, make a polite remark such as, "Please wait a moment while I check the record for you." If you are delayed in finding the desired information, offer to call back. If the caller prefers to hold the line, put down the receiver gently to avoid an unpleasant noise in his ear.

If the caller speaks at length, do not interrupt. Be patient, listen attentively, and never ask him to repeat unless there is mechanical distortion on the line or some other good reason for your inability to hear. Never talk with a pencil, chewing gum, or cigarette in your mouth. When the call is finished, say good-bye in a pleasant tone and replace the receiver quietly after the caller has hung up.

Use the telephone directory when necessary, but do not hesitate to dial Information for numbers not found in the directory.

Before placing a call, decide what you intend to say; be sure of what your purpose is, and have all pertinent information before you. Be brief, but not curt. Use friendly expressions throughout the conversation, remembering that your listener cannot see the smile on your face but can only judge you by the words you speak and your manner of speaking them.

After dialing, let the signal ring at least ten times. Upon hearing an answer, identify yourself immediately: "This is Miss Scott with John A. Brown Company." If your call is going through a switchboard at the other end, ask for the person you want to speak with and identify yourself at the same time: "May I speak with Miss Henderson in the Ladies Ready-to-Wear Department, please? Miss Scott of John A. Brown Company calling."

If you are not calling a particular person by name, state your purpose in a succinct manner: "Will you please connect me with the department that sells electric skillets?"

When answering an incoming call, if there is not a switchboard, state the name of your company and your own name: "John A. Brown Company, Miss Robertson." If there is a switchboard and the operator has already answered the call before ringing your extension, state your department and your name: "Ladies Ready-to-Wear Department, Miss Henderson speaking." If there is no department, give only your name: "Miss Henderson speaking."

When answering a colleague's extension, state the colleague's name and your own: "Miss Henderson's office, Miss Scott speaking." If the person called is not readily available, ask the caller if he wishes to hold the line, to leave a message, or to call back. If he prefers to hold the line, go back on the line at short intervals to explain the delay, asking if he wishes to leave a message.

When taking a message, ask for the name of the caller, his company, and his telephone number, making a notation of the time of the call. Be sure that the person called receives the message as soon as he returns to his desk.

Do not transfer a call if you yourself can take care of the matter properly. Otherwise: "Mr. Jack Phillips is in charge of insurance, and I am sure he will advise you promptly." If you do not immediately know to whom the call should be referred, tell the caller: "I shall have the proper person call you back in a few minutes."

Always advise your switchboard operator of the situation so that she will not have to ask the caller for additional information: "Please connect Mr. Brown with Mr. Phillips in the Insurance Department." Or if the caller has not identified himself: "Please transfer this call to Mr. Phillips in the Insurance Department."

When answering a call for your employer and hearing the caller's secretary on the line, say, "Thank you. Just a moment, please." Then announce the call to your employer. He will pick up the phone (if he is courteous) and will wait until the person calling him is connected. Never ask the calling secretary to put her employer on the line first, unless your employer is a high-ranking personage requiring special consideration.

On the other hand, when *you* place a call for your employer, you are in the position of having the secretary of the person being called put her employer on the line before you connect your own employer. If you are calling Mr. Fisk and his secretary answers, say, "Is Mr. Fisk there, please, for Mr. Brown of John A. Brown Company?" If Mr. Fisk's secretary knows her business she will then put Mr. Fisk on the line, and you will say to your employer, "Mr. Fisk is on the line, Mr. Brown."

If Mr. Fisk's secretary is not cooperative, continue to speak courteously and explain to your employer that the other secretary insists that he go on the line before she connects Mr. Fisk.

If your employer asks you to screen his calls, do so in an extremely tactful manner. Otherwise the caller may be easily affronted. Say, "May I tell Mr. Jones who is calling?" This should encourage the caller to give his name without hesitation. If he refuses, explain to him that your employer is unable to accept the call and suggest that he write. A secretary must be the judge as to whether or not her employer should be disturbed. But she must be prepared to meet the caller face-to-face the next day without feeling embarrassed about the way she treated him over the phone.

Often-Used Numbers

There are certain numbers that your employer uses regularly, and no doubt the secretary will soon memorize them without effort. But she will do well to keep a short alphabetical list of them close to her telephone, so that she can consult it without an instant's hesitation. This list could include her employer's garage, the schools where his children are, the stores where his wife has charge accounts, his tailor, his clubs, and his personal friends with whom he and his wife exchange evening entertainments.

The telephone numbers opposite each name should include the area codes of exchanges not in your immediate area. For long-distance areas note the time differentials between the other cities and your own, to avoid trying to reach an associate when he is having a good night's sleep.

Some secretaries leave a list of this kind fitted beneath the desk blotter's cellophane cover, or taped to a pull-out shelf of the desk. However, there are reasons for keeping the desk uncluttered, and it may be good to avoid this.

If your employer frequently uses certain business telephone numbers, you ought to have a new card-operated dial telephone. For this device the numbers most used are coded on perforated cards. By merely placing a card in the special slot you can see the number dialed automatically.

Connections

If your employer is likely to go on inspection trips throughout a large plant and you sometimes have difficulty in reaching him when an important telephone call comes in, ask him to equip himself with a portable receiver that will fit into his pocket. Then you can buzz him, and he can pick up the nearest telephone to enable you to connect him. If it turns out to be important for you to converse with him while he is going from one department to another, he may decide to install a walkie-talkie connection.

If you sometimes find it hard to obtain an answer to an extension when your employer has asked you to connect him with one of the managers of the various departments, by dialing a special extension you can set off automatic paging throughout the plant. When your voice penetrates the air—"Paging Mr. Lawrence for Mr. Bronson"—Mr. Lawrence will reach the nearest phone and ask for Mr. Bronson's extension.

Long-Distance Calls

The secretary will often be asked to place long-distance calls.

A station-to-station call is made from one telephone directly to another telephone when the caller is willing to talk with anyone who may answer. Charges for the call begin when an answer is heard. This is considerably cheaper than a person-to-person call but should be used only when you are relatively sure that anyone who answers can be of service to you. Direct dialing is possible to most stations.

Charges for a person-to-person call do not begin to accrue until the person called answers. This service is more expensive than a station-to-station call but may prove to be more economical if you are not sure the person you are calling will be at the telphone.

In placing a long-distance call, give the operator the name of the town or city you are calling, together with the telephone number. If you are calling person-to-person, give the name of the person. If you expect the person being called to pay for the call, say, "This is a collect call. My name is Miss Scott of John A. Brown Company." If you are willing to speak to a second person when the first mentioned is not available, give this information to the operator before she places the call. If you have reason to believe that the person called may be at another telephone number or in another city, explain all that as well: "If Mr. Greene is not at 778-1860 please try 843-1960."

Conference Calls

In placing a conference call, on which as many persons as desired may talk, ask for the conference operator and give her the names and telephone numbers of the persons to be convened. When all of them are on the line the operator will connect you, and the charge will begin at that time.

Overseas and Ship-to-Shore Calls

You may call any country in the world or a ship at sea (if the ship has facilities for receiving the call), merely by asking for the overseas operator or ship-to-shore operator.

New Devices

The telephone company will advise you how to increase the efficiency of the telephone service in your company. You may be able to use some of their devices with which you are not familiar, and an inquiry will be worthwhile. Ask about switching, hold buttons, exclusion buttons, cut-off, pickup, audible signal, visual signal, speaker-phone sets, automatic answering and recording sets, and intercommunicating features.

The old-time buzzer used to summon a secretary can now be replaced by an intercommunicating device that enables the employer to speak to her as though she were in the room with him, and she can reply just as comfortably.

Telegraph

Messages can be sent by wire to any point in the United States, Mexico, and Canada. Messages to other points will be discussed under the heading *Cablegrams.*

You may send a straight telegram, a day letter, or a night letter. The straight telegram is the fastest service aside from the telephone. Charges are based on a minimum of fifteen words with an added charge for each word above fifteen. Address and signature are not counted as words.

Transmission of a day letter may be delayed until all straight telegrams have been dispatched. Charge is based on a minimum of fifty words and on each additional group of five words. Day letter charges are forty percent higher than the minimum charge for a straight telegram. Thus, if your message is fifteen words or less it is cheaper to use the straight service.

The night letter is the slowest and least expensive. It may be recorded at any time up to 2:00 A.M. and is delivered the morning of the following day. Charges are computed the same as for day letters, based on a minimum of fifty words with an additional charge for each group of five words above fifty. Address and signature are not counted as words. Unlike the cost of a day letter, the cost of a fifty-word night letter is less than the cost of a fifteen-word straight telegram.

Usually an office requires four copies of a telegram to be

typed: an original for the Western Union messenger to pick up when he comes at your request from the nearest Western Union office; a confirmation copy to be mailed to the addressee; a file copy; and the copy needed by the accounting department.

On the Western Union standard form, type an X in the blank denoting the kind of service ordered. Type the date and hour in spaces provided in the upper right corner. No salutation or complimentary close is used. The message should be double-spaced for easy reading, and no division of words should be made. In the lower left corner of the blank, indicate *Charge* (when your company has a charge account with Western Union), *Paid* (when you are paying for the wire at the time of sending it), or *Collect* (when charges are to be collected from the addressee at the time of delivery). Insert also the sender's name and address.

Multiple Messages

If the same message is to be delivered to more than one person, type the message only once, then list the names and addresses on a special form obtained from Western Union, or on a plain sheet of paper, marked, "Send the attached message to each of the following."

Train Delivery

On a message to be delivered to someone on a train, give the name, train number or name, direction the train is traveling, car and reservation number (if known), station and arrival time, city, and state. Also show that the message is to be delivered in care of the conductor of the train:

> Mr. Philip W. Wade
> Care of Conductor
> The Twentieth Century Limited, Westbound
> Car 9, Bedroom 22
> Due at LaSalle Street Station
> Chicago, Illinois
> May 5, 10:30 P.M.

Airport Delivery

On a message sent to an airport for delivery to a plane passenger, show the name, the airline, the flight number, direction of travel, airport, arrival time, city, and state:

Mr. Philip W. Wade
A Passenger
American Airlines
Flight 88, Northbound
Due at Midway Airport
Chicago, Illinois
May 5, 12:00 noon.

Telefax or Desk-Fax

A device is obtainable from Western Union that can dispatch a message immediately after it is typed, without a messenger's call. A special blank is provided, the message is typed within the allotted lines and then placed on a revolving drum and photographed, the picture being received at once at the Western Union office. In the same manner, incoming telegrams can be read directly from the picture transmitted to your office by the Western Union office.

Consult your nearest Western Union for information concerning this service.

Money Orders

You may send money by telegraph to any point in the United States and to many countries in the world. Deposit the amount of money you wish to send at any Western Union office; it will promptly be delivered to the recipient.

Errand Service

Western Union messengers are available for practically every type of errand such as the pickup and delivery of packages, papers, documents, or any article that can be carried conveniently.

Cablegrams

Communications to foreign countries can go as full-rate messages (abbreviated FR), equivalent to straight telegraph service. Messages may be sent in ordinary language or in code. Charge per word is based on distance to destination, not exceeding thirty cents a word (minimum five words). Contrary to custom in domestic telegraph service, the address, signature, figures, and signs are each counted as a word.

Letter telegrams (LT) are similar to domestic night letters and are dispatched at the full rate, delivery made on an overnight basis as with a night letter. Code is not accepted for letter telegrams; they must be written only in the language of the country of origin. The charge for each word is one-half the full rate (minimum twenty-two words), and digits are counted as words.

Ship-to-Shore

Ship-to-shore or shore-to-ship service is available from any Western Union office. Give the addressee's name, the ship, the nearest radio station, if known, and mark the message INTL:

> INTL
> John Sidney Roberts
> SS UNITED STATES
> Portsmouth, England.

Code is acceptable; address and signature and INTL are counted as words.

Economy in Wording

You can save money for your employer by using care in preparing a telegram or cablegram.

> *Example:*
>
> WIRE US ALL THE DATA YOU HAVE ON PRICES OF STEEL GRAIN BINS SO THAT WE WILL HAVE IT BY NOON MONDAY. DO NOT SEND FREIGHT CHARGES.
>
> *Improvement:*
>
> WIRE DATA ON STEEL BIN PRICES BY NOON MONDAY. FREIGHT CHARGES UNNECESSARY.

Fourteen words are in this case saved by rearrangement of the words, and the clear message, less than fifteen words, can be sent at the minimum rate.

Express

Anything can be shipped by express, from a paper clip to a giraffe. Railroads provide appropriate cars for special articles, some utilizing side doors, others end doors, for ease in loading. Specially constructed cars are provided for valuable racehorses, livestock, and other animals. When live creatures are shipped, a suitable crate must be provided, with feeding and watering instructions attached to the crate, which must be of ample size to allow the animal to travel in comfort. For the shipping of perishable goods a refrigerated car is used.

Railway Express maintains a pickup and delivery service in or near practically every city and town in the United States. Look up Railway Express (or REA) in your telephone directory, dial the number, and ask for Pickup Service. When the Railway Express driver collects the shipment he will prepare an express receipt in duplicate, leaving the original with you. When the shipment is delivered, a receipt is obtained from the consignee.

By Air

Express charges include valuation coverage free up to fifty dollars for shipments weighing one hundred pounds or less, fifty cents a pound for anything over one hundred pounds. Because rates are subject to change, it is advisable to check with your local express agency before making a shipment.

The Railway Express Agency provides air express service, as do a number of airlines. This service is available to more than twenty-two thousand communities not serviced by an airline, by means of coordinated rail-truck ground facilities. Therefore every city in the United States, Canada, Mexico, and South America can be reached in a matter of hours. In large cities there is special delivery of air express shipments on a twenty-four-hour basis, even on Sundays and holidays. Air express shipments can be sent prepaid or collect.

Collection Service

On an express shipment sent C.O.D. the shipping charges are collected from the consignee upon delivery. Even the cost of the article itself can be collected and remitted to the shipper. Installment payments, checks, accounts, drafts, and bills are also handled for collection by Railway Express. They will pick up merchandise covered by an invoice and dispose of it according to the shipper's instructions.

United States Post Office

There are several classes of mail service: sealed letters—first class, registered, and (if requested) returned with a signed receipt from the addressee. Printed periodicals—second class. Books, drawings, photographs, circulars, parcels, and plants—third class. Manuscripts—fourth class (insured if desired). There are special rates for postcards, unsealed greeting cards, and announcements, as well as for bulk mailings and educational material.

Whatever your company's particular mailing problem is, your nearest postmaster will be able to suggest the department's best method for you.

VII

Your Native Language

Mankind's greatest source of expansion is in expression, and for every idea expressed a new series of ideas bursts forth. Give careful attention to the correct use of your native language. As you improve your speech you will also improve your personal life and your business success.

Words, phrases, and sentences that are outworn ought not to be used in a business letter. Stock phrases are, like slang, used only when the writer is too lethargic to think his idea through and to choose the best language for expressing it. It is necessary first to understand thoroughly what you want to say and then to say it forcefully with words as natural to you as they would be in a personal interview. This will help you accomplish the purpose of communication.

To help yourself write naturally, consider how you would respond to a luncheon invitation from an acquaintance. Would you say, "In accordance with your request that I have lunch with you, I beg to advise that I shall be happy to do so." No. You would be more likely to say, "Thanks. I'll be glad to lunch with you."

Verbose Expressions

You ought to be alert to everything you write—without having to take a course in semantics, which would merely emphasize the folly of using a word that does not mean exactly what you want it to say. As examples of pitfalls to avoid, the following partial list explains how a letter writer can win a reputation for carelessness or vagueness. After studying this list protect yourself from similar mistakes.

Verbose Expressions	*What You Really Mean*
I beg to be advised	Please tell me
Thank you kindly	Thank you
I feel that you are able to appreciate	You can appreciate
Which you will remember is in connection with	Regarding
I am not at present in a position	I am unable
I would, therefore, ask that you kindly write	Please write
We would appreciate it if you would investigate the matter and inform us	Please check the matter and report
You have my permission to	You may
I am in receipt of a complaint from John Smith	John Smith complains
You have not, I believe, favored us with a reply	You have not replied
I acknowledge receipt of your kind letter	I received your letter

Correct Usage

Aside from indulgence in verbosity, many letter writers frequently misuse parts of speech. The following examples are given to alert the reader to many other such mistakes that may come to mind when he develops that habit of speaking precisely.

Nouns

bushel—
> *Wrong*: Eight bushel of oats
> *Right*: Eight bushels of oats

business—
> *Wrong*: What business is it of theirs to question my action?
> *Right*: What right have they to question my action?

combination—
> *Wrong*: That combine will be a large one.
> *Right*: That combination will be a large one.

council, counsel, consul—
> A *council* is a group of persons convened for advisory purposes.
> *Counsel* is advice; sometimes means *attorney*.
> A *consul* is an official appointed by a government to report on matters he observes while residing in a foreign land.

data—
> always plural

era—
> pronounced *ee'-rah*, never like *error*

foot or feet—
> *Wrong*: The room is twelve foot long.
> *Right*: The room is twelve feet long.

kind—
> *Wrong*: She asked for those kind of flowers.
> *Right*: She asked for that kind of flowers.

loan—
> *Wrong*: Loan me your pen.
> *Right*: Lend me your pen.
> *Right*: He went to the bank to make a loan.

lots—
> *Wrong*: She receives lots of fan mail.
> *Right*: She receives a great deal of fan mail.

majority—
>*Wrong*: The majority of the work is finished.
>*Right*: The larger part of the work is finished.
>*Right*: The majority of his constituents voted for him.
>*Right*: John reached his majority last week.

party—
>*Wrong*: The party I called was disturbed.
>*Right*: The person I called was disturbed.
>*Right* (in legal documents): The party of the second part hereby agrees ...
>*Right*: He celebrated his birthday with a party.
>*Right*: The Republican party waged a strong campaign.

people—
>*Wrong*: The General Motors people
>*Right*: The people of Massachusetts

per cent (two words following an amount)—
>*Right*: Six per cent interest was charged.

percentage (when no amount is given)—
>*Right*: What percentage of interest was charged?

proposal (an offer)—
>*Right*: Did you consider his proposal?

proposition (a matter discussed)—
>*Right*: We intend to consider his proposition.

shape (meaning tangible form)—
>*Wrong*: The transaction was completed in good shape.
>*Right*: The transaction was completed to everyone's satisfaction.

suspicion (noun)—
>*Wrong*: They suspicion that he murdered a man.
>*Right*: They suspect that he murdered a man.

Pronouns

any, either—
>*any* refers to one of several
>*either* refers to one of two

Right: You may have any of the six books.
Right: Either of those two cars will be acceptable.
Pronouns must agree in number and person with the words to which they have reference.

each, their—
Wrong: Each drives their own car.
Right: Each drives his own car.
Right: Each of the women listed *her* needs. (Not: *their* needs.)

one—
Wrong: One likes to see their time constructively used.
Right: One likes to use his time constructively.

its, it's—
its is a possessive pronoun
it's is a contraction meaning *it is*

Right: It's getting dark.
Right: The ship was flying its flag at half-mast.

I—
nominative case, never the object of a preposition

Wrong: Just between you and I
Right: Just between you and me
Wrong: He asked that the money be given to you and I.
Right: He asked that the money be given to you and me.

she—
nominative case, never the object of a preposition

Wrong: I will give the money to you and she.
Right: I will give the money to you and her.

he—
nominative case, never the object of a preposition

Wrong: I will give the money to you and he.
Right: I will give the money to you and him.

they—
nominative case, never the object of a preposition

Wrong: I will give the money to you and they.
Right: I will give the money to you and them.
Wrong: You and them are welcome to come.
Right: You and they are welcome to come.

we—
nominative case, always used as subject of a sentence

Wrong: Us boys are ready to play the game.
Right: We boys are ready to play the game.

same—
Wrong: Your letter arrived and I acknowledge same with thanks.
Right: Your letter arrived and I acknowledge it with thanks.

which—
a relative pronoun, must have a noun or a pronoun as its antecedent, can never refer to a whole situation described in a clause or phrase

Wrong: He did not arrive in time for the meeting, which caused the president embarrassment.
Right: His failure to arrive in time for the meeting caused the president embarrassment.
Right: His failure to arrive, which caused the president embarrassment, was the reason for his discharge.

(See also "restrictive and nonrestrictive clauses" in any book on modern usage.)

Conjunctions

because—
Wrong: The reason he did not attend the party is because he was in Chicago.
Right: He did not attend the party because he was in Chicago.
Right: The reason he did not attend the party is that he was in Chicago.

except, unless—
   except is a preposition used to introduce a prepositional phrase
   unless is an adverbial conjunction used to introduce a subordinate clause

   Wrong: The horse cannot be entered in the race except the judges permit.
   Right: The horse cannot be entered in the race unless the judges permit.
   Right: No horses can be entered in the race except those permitted by the judges.

like, as—
   like is a preposition always followed by a noun or pronoun in the objective case
   as is an adverbial conjunction used to introduce a subordinate clause

   Wrong: It appears like he isn't coming.
   Right: It appears as if he isn't coming.
   Right: Though he was such a little boy he marched like a major.

who, which, that—
   Right: She is the woman who smiled at him.
   Right: She is the kind of person that everyone likes.
   Right: That is the book on Homer which I lost.

Prepositions

between, among—
   between is used to differentiate two objects
   among is used to differentiate more than two

   Right: The dog was sitting between John and me.
   Right: There were three good books among the many he gave me.

off—
   Wrong: The ribbon was taken off of the package.
   Right: The ribbon was taken off the package.
   Wrong: He bought the house off of John Smith.
   Right: He bought the house from John Smith.

to *and* at (not used with where)—
   Wrong: Where are you at?

Right: Where are you?
Wrong: Where did he go to?
Right: Where did he go?

Adjectives and Adverbs

aged—
pronounced *ayj-èd* when an adjective
pronounced one syllable when used as a verb, especially as a past participle

Wrong: Medicare is supposed to relieve the ag'd (ayjd) of heavy expense.
Right: Medicare is supposed to relieve the aged (ayj-èd) of heavy expense.
Right: A gentleman aged (ayjd) about sixty years came to the platform to speak in favor of reducing taxes for the aged (ayj-èd).

already, all ready—
Right: She had already arrived.
Right: We are all ready to leave.

all right (always two words)—
Right: It will be all right if you wish to go.

altogether, all together—
Right: She is altogether pleasant.
Right: The books were all together on one shelf.

only—
Wrong: I could only get him to play one piece.
Right: I could get him to play only one piece.

very—
very is not ordinarily used to modify a past participle directly.
Wrong: She was very displeased.
Right: She was very much displeased.

where—
Wrong: Did you read in the paper where our mayor was honored at a banquet?
Right: Did you read in the paper that our mayor was honored at a banquet?

Verbs

bring, take—
Right: Bring me the book.
Right: Take the book to him.

can't seem—
Wrong: I can't seem to make the journey in an hour.
Right: It seems impossible for me to make the journey in one hour.

cooperate—
Wrong: If they cooperate together, their purpose will be accomplished.
Right: If they cooperate, their purpose will be accomplished.

dangling participles—
Wrong: Walking down Main Street, the art museum is visible.
(This gives the impression that the art museum is walking down Main Street.)
Right: Walking down Main Street, one can see the art museum.
(The participial phrase must modify the noun or pronoun to which it refers.)

don't—
Wrong: He don't (do not) care to go with us.
Right: He doesn't (does not) care to go with us.

enthuse—
Wrong: He was enthused over winning the award.
Right: He was enthusiastic over winning the award.

expect—
Wrong: I expect she was well received.
Right: I suppose she was well received.
Right: I expect her to come early.

got—
Wrong: I have got a new car.
Right: I have a new car.
Right: He got a new job.
Wrong: I've got to stop at his house.

Right: I must stop at his house, *or* I have to stop at his house.

gotten (obsolete)

guess—
Wrong: I guess you are right.
Right: I think you are right.
Right: In the word game, Alfred was the first to guess correctly.
Right: Alfred made the right guess.

had of (or had've)—
Wrong: If you had of mentioned it I would of gone.
Right: If you had mentioned it to me, I would have gone.

inaugurate—
Wrong: The program was inaugurated on August 1.
Right: The President was inaugurated on January 4.
Right: The program was begun on August 1.

inside of, within—
Wrong: He will visit us inside of a week.
Right: He will visit us within a week.

learn, teach—
Wrong: He learned me how to type.
Right: She taught me how to type.
Right: If I teach him correctly, he will learn quickly.

let, leave—
let means to permit
leave means to depart, to bequeath, or to allow to remain

Wrong: Leave her go with us.
Right: Let her go with us.
Right: I shall leave this to you when I die.
Right: Leave your dog with me while you are on your vacation.

lie, lay—
Lie is intransitive (no object accompanies it). *Lie* means to remain in position or to rest. *Lie* is active. *Lay* is

transitive and an object always accompanies it. *Lay* means to place something somewhere.

> *Wrong*: He lays down after lunch every day.
> *Right*: He lies down after lunch every day.
> *Right*: Will you please lay the book on the table?
> *Right*: He lay on the couch yesterday because he was
tired.
> *Right*: The pen lay on the desk all day.

may, can—
> *Right*: May I go with you?
> *Right*: Can he drive a car?

open up—
> *Wrong*: We open up the doors promptly at noon.
> *Right*: We open the doors promptly at noon.

raise, rise—
> *Right*: They raise the question at every meeting.
> *Right*: I rise to make a motion.

shall, will—
Use *shall* to express expected action with first person, *will* with second and third persons.

> *Right*: I shall go tomorrow.
> *Wrong*: He shall go tomorrow.
> *Right*: He will go tomorrow.
> *Right*: Shall I go too?
> *Wrong*: Shall he go too?
> *Right*: Will he go too?
> *Right*: You will go with us, won't you?

Use *should* with first person, *would* with second and third persons to express expected action, as with *shall* and *will*. Using *should* and *would* instead of *shall* and *will* implies a doubt that the action will take place.

> *Right*: I should appreciate hearing from you.
> *Wrong*: I would appreciate hearing from you.
> *Right*: You would appreciate hearing from her.
> *Right*: Should I go with you?
> *Right*: Would he go with me?
> *Wrong*: Should he go with me?
> *Right*: I should like to see the game.
> *Right*: She would like to see the game.

sit, set—

Right: She sits near her husband at every meeting.

Right: She sets the plates on the table in an orderly manner.

Right: She sets the hen and hopes the eggs will be hatched.

Additional Examples

above—

Wrong: Please reread the above statement.

Right: Please reread the foregoing (*or* preceding) statement.

affect, effect—

Right: The light affects my vision.

Right: The decoration made a brilliant effect.

Right: Can you effect a change in the operation?

and—

(the conjunction that joins coordinate clauses or two parts of speech of equal value)

Right: The meeting will be held Tuesday, and the vice-president will preside.

Right: Stenographers and other personnel are entitled to use the cafeteria.

awful—

Wrong: Bill is awfully smart.

Right: Bill is unusually smart.

Wrong: She performed an awful task.

Right: She performed a difficult task.

a while, awhile—

Right: Relax awhile before you begin the task.

Right: Please come to my home for a while before you start your journey.

badly—

Wrong: He wanted badly to go with them.

Right: He wanted very much to go with them.

Wrong: She felt badly after her operation.

Right: She did not feel well after her operation.

both alike—
Wrong: The cars are both alike.
Right: The two cars are alike. They are both of the latest model.

both, each—
Wrong: There is a picture on both sides of the mantel.
Right: There is a picture on each side of the mantel.

came by—
Wrong: He came by to see me.
Right: He came to see me.

credible, credulous—
Right: He related the incident in a credible manner.
Right: She is too credulous for her own good.

deal—
Wrong: She made a deal to buy the house.
Right: She made an agreement to buy the house.

different—
Wrong: That is a different road than the one I followed yesterday.
Right: That is a different road from the one I followed yesterday.

either, neither—
Wrong: Neither of the four books suited him.
Right: None of the four books suited him.
Wrong: Either of the three books is the one I want.
Right: Either of the two books will do.
Right: Any of the three books will suit me.

else (in possessive form)—
Right: She thinks her job is more important than anybody else's.

farther, further—
Right: I walked farther than he did.
Right: He will go further with your help than without it.

fix—
    Wrong: She is in a desperate fix.
    Right: She is desperate because of her present situation.

invite—
    Wrong: I have an invite to the party.
    Right: I have an invitation to the party.

kind of, sort of—
    Wrong: He appeared to be kind of ill.
    Right: He appeared to be rather ill.
    Wrong: She was sort of ill at ease.
    Right: She was somewhat ill at ease.

less, fewer—
    Right: This mine contains less gold than the Jackass Mine.
    Right: This city has fewer people today than it had one year ago.

lost—
    Wrong: He lost out.
    Right: He lost.

liable, likely—
    Right: The landlord is liable for damages.
    Right: That horse is likely to win the race.

line—
    Wrong: He is in the drug line.
    Right: He is in the drug business.

mad, angry—
    Wrong: Mary was mad at Jane.
    Right: Mary was angry with Jane.

most, almost—
    Wrong: We walked most all the way.
    Right: We walked almost all the way.

never—
    Wrong: We never saw your dog since yesterday.
    Right: We have not seen your dog since yesterday.
    Right: We never saw your dog. What breed was he?

posted, informed—
Wrong: You are well-posted on the subject.
Right: You are well-informed about Australia.

pretend—
Wrong: Pretend like you want to go.
Right: Pretend that you want to go.

real—
Wrong: He is real handsome.
Right: He is very handsome.

run—
Wrong: He runs the bakery.
Right: He manages the bakery.

so—
Avoid overuse of this adverbial conjunction. *Consequently, therefore, inasmuch as* are good substitutes when you want to vary the style.

sometime, some time—
Right: I will go sometime this morning.
Right: If I have some time this morning, I shall do the job for you.

try and, come and, be sure and—
Wrong: Try and be here at noon.
Right: Try to be here at noon.
Wrong: Come and see me tomorrow.
Right: Come to see me tomorrow.
Wrong: Be sure and watch out as you cross the street.
Right: Be sure to watch out as you cross the street.

wait on—
Wrong: Please do not wait on me if I am not at the station when you arrive.
Right: Please do not wait for me if I am not there when you arrive.
Right: The headwaiter assigned the red-haired girl to wait on me.

VIII
Spelling

The constant study of spelling and the exact meaning of words is an important aspect of a secretary's career. A dictionary is her most effective aid, for it provides information such as:

> syllabication (useful when you want to split a word at the end of a typewritten line)
> variant spellings, with preferred spelling shown
> pronunciations, with preferred form shown
> capitalization
> hyphenation
> italicization
> parts of speech
> plurals of nouns
> cases of pronouns
> verb tenses
> comparative and superlative forms of irregular adverbs and adjectives
> derivations of words
> synonyms and antonyms
> status labels if colloquial, archaic, obsolete, etc.

Some of the words whose spelling frequently puzzles many of us are discussed in this chapter in order to sharpen the reader's awareness of spelling in general.

Plurals

1. The general rule is to form the plural of a noun by adding *s*:

book	books
clock	clocks
pen	pens

2. A noun ending in *o* preceded by a vowel takes an *s* for the plural:

curio	curios
folio	folios
radio	radios
ratio	ratios
studio	studios

Some singular nouns ending in *o*, preceded by a consonant, take *es* to form the plural, while others take *s*:

banjo	banjos
buffalo	buffaloes
cargo	cargoes
Eskimo	Eskimos
hero	heroes
mosquito	mosquitoes
motto	mottoes
piano	pianos
potato	potatoes
soprano	sopranos
tomato	tomatoes

3. A singular noun ending in *ch, sh, s, x,* or *z* takes *es* for the plural:

bush	bushes
chintz	chintzes
dress	dresses
inch	inches
wax	waxes

4. A noun ending in *y* preceded by a consonant changes the *y* to *i* and adds *es* for the plural:

ability	abilities
auxiliary	auxiliaries
discrepancy	discrepancies
facility	facilities
industry	industries
lady	ladies
society	societies

5. A noun ending in *y* preceded by a vowel takes only an *s* for the plural:

attorney	attorneys
galley	galleys
kidney	kidneys
monkey	monkeys
turkey	turkeys

6. Some plurals end in *en*:

child	children
man	men
ox	oxen

7. Some nouns ending in *f* or *fe* change the *f* or *fe* to *v* and add *es* for the plural:

calf	calves
knife	knives
leaf	leaves
life	lives
loaf	loaves
shelf	shelves

Some Exceptions:

bailiff	bailiffs
belief	beliefs
chief	chiefs
gulf	gulfs
roof	roofs

8. Some nouns require a vowel change for the plural:

foot	feet
goose	geese
mouse	mice
tooth	teeth

9. The plural of numerals, signs, and letters is shown by adding an apostrophe and *s*:

> C.O.D.'s
> the 80's
> four B's

10. To proper names ending in *s* or in an *s* sound, add *es* for the plural:

Brooks	the Brookses
Burns	the Burnses
Jones	the Joneses

11. A compound noun, when hyphenated or when consisting of two separate words, shows the plural form in the most important element:

attorney-in-fact	attorneys-in-fact
brigadier general	brigadier generals
brother-in-law	brothers-in-law
notary public	notaries public

12. The plural of solid compounds (a compound noun written as one word) is formed at the end of the solid compound:

bookshelf	bookshelves
cupful	cupfuls
lumberman	lumbermen
stepchild	stepchildren
stepdaughter	stepdaughters

13. Some nouns are written the same for singular and plural:

> Chinese
> corps
> deer
> salmon
> sheep
> vermin
> wheat

14. Some nouns always appear as singular:

> civics
> mathematics
> measles
> milk

> molasses
> music
> news
> statistics

15. Some nouns always appear as plural:

> pants
> proceeds
> remains
> riches
> scissors
> thanks
> trousers
> tweezers

The Suffix

1. Words whose roots end with *ge* or *ce* generally retain the *e* when a suffix is added:

change	changeable
damage	damageable
disadvantage	disadvantageous
outrage	outrageous

2. A final silent *e* is usually dropped before a suffix that begins with a vowel:

argue	arguing
change	changing
conceive	conceivable

3. A final silent *e* is usually retained before a suffix that begins with a consonant:

achieve	achievement
definite	definitely

4. In words ending in *c*, add *k* before a suffix beginning with *e*, *i*, or *y*, so that the hard sound of the original *c* is retained:

frolic	frolicked	frolicking
mimic	mimicked	mimicking
picnic	picnicked	picnicking

5. A word ending in *ie* changes the *ie* to *y* when adding a suffix:

die	dying
lie	lying
tie	tying
vie	vying

6. Words that end in *y* preceded by a vowel retain the *y* when adding the suffix:

survey   surveying   surveyor

7. Words that end with *y* preceded by a consonant change *y* to *i* when adding a suffix, except when the suffix is "ing."

embody	embodying
rely	relying
satisfy	satisfying

8. A final consonant is usually doubled when it is preceded by a single vowel and takes a suffix:

mop   mopping

9. A final consonant is doubled when it is followed by a suffix and the last syllable is accented:

acquit   acquitted

10. The final consonant is *not* doubled when the accent is shifted to a preceding syllable when the suffix is added:

refer   referring   *but* reference

or when the final consonant is preceded by two vowels:

toil   toiling

or when the final consonant is preceded by another consonant:

fold   folding

11. Irregular spellings to watch closely:

acknowledgment
awful
judgment

> ninth
> truly
> wholly

12. Words ending in ceed, cede, and sede:

> exceed
> intercede
> precede
> proceed
> recede
> secede
> succeed
> supersede

Memorize: The only English word that ends in *sede* is *supersede*. The only English words that end in *ceed* are *exceed, proceed,* and *succeed.*

Capitalization

Proper nouns that denote the names of specific persons or places are capitalized, though names that are common to a group are not.

Acts and laws of Congress are capitalized:

> the Civil Rights Bill
> the Labor Relations Law
> the Taft-Hartley Act

Amendments to the Constitution are capitalized only if they are referred to by number or title. When referred to generally thy are not capitalized:

> the recent amendment to the Constitution
> the Child Labor Amendment
> the Eighteenth Amendment

Associations:

> Society of Professional Engineers
> American Business Association
> Young Women's Christian Association

Books and their subdivisions:

> *The American Way,* Chapter VI
> *Remembrance of Things Past,* Volume II

Bulletins and periodical titles:

> *The New York Retail Bulletin*
> *The Wall Street Journal*

Cars of railroads and automobile manufacturers:

> Car 54, Train 93
> Plymouth
> Cadillac

Churches and church dignitaries:

> Fifth Avenue Presbyterian Church
> the Archbishop of New York
> Bishop John Barnes

Cities:

> Jefferson City, Missouri
> Los Angeles, California
> (*but*—the city of Los Angeles)
> The city was clouded with smog.

Clubs:

> Possum Kingdom Club
> The Do-Gooders
> The Union League Club
> (*but*—many Republican clubs in the West)

Codes:

> the Code of Building Maintenance
> (*but*—the building code)
> Code VII

Compass points that designate a specific region:

> the Northeast (section of the country)
> the Pacific Northwest
> northwest (direction)
> toward the south
> east of town

Constitutions:

>   the Constitution of Texas
>   the Constitution of the United States
>   (*but*—the constitution of any free nation)

Corporations:

>   the American Brake Corporation
>   the Container Corporation of America
>   (*but*—The corporation was dissolved.)

Courts:

>   the Criminal Court of Appeals
>   (*but*—a court of appeals)
>   the Supreme Court
>   the Magistrate's Court
>   (*but*—a county court)

Decorations:

>   the Purple Heart
>   the Good Conduct Medal
>   the Croix de Guerre
>   (*but*—Soldiers are given decorations to
>   signal their acts of heroism.)

Degrees (Academic):

>   D.D.
>   M.D.
>   LL.D.
>   Ph.D.

District:

>   the First Congressional District
>   (*but*—a congressional district)

Educational courses:

>   English II
>   Spanish Grammar
>   (*but*—He is studying physics and chemistry.)

Epithets:

>   the First Lady of the State
>   Alexander the Great

Fleets:

the Third Fleet
(*but*—The ship was part of the fleet.)

Foundations:

the Carnegie Foundation
the Ford Foundation
(*but*—He established a foundation.)

Geographical divisions:

the Lone Star State
the Sooner State
(*but*—There are fifty states in our country.)
Northern Hemisphere
South Pole
the Old World
the Near East

Government divisions:

the Federal Reserve Board
the Fire Department
(*but*—The department was headed by
Mr. Charles Bleeker.)

Historical terms:

the Dark Ages
the Renaissance
the Christian Era
World War II
the Battle of the Bulge
the Declaration of Independence
the Magna Carta

Holidays:

Thanksgiving Day
Passover
Easter Sunday
New Year's Eve

Libraries:

the Carnegie Library
the Dallas Public Library
(*but*—The library is a source of information.)

Localities:

> Western Europe
> East Africa
> the Wheat Belt
> the West Side
> the Mississippi Delta

Military services:

> the United States Navy
> the Signal Corps
> the Second Battalion
> Company B

Nobility and Royalty:

> the Queen of Belgium
>   (*but*—Many a queen was honored here.)
> the Duke of Windsor
>   (*but*—She was proud to have met a duke.)

Oceans and continents:

> the Pacific Ocean
>   (*but*—He was glad to be crossing the ocean.)
> the Red Sea
> North America
> Antarctica

Parks:

> Greenleaf Park
> Texoma State Park
> Yosemite National Park
>   (*but*—The park was in the southern part of the state.)

Personification:

> He was recognized by the Chair and
>   spoke briefly.
> He sang about Summer in all her glory.
>   (*but*—In the summer the days are longer.)

Planets and other heavenly bodies:

> Mars
> Venus

the Big Dipper
    (*but*—The moon rises late tonight.)

Races, tribes, and peoples:

> Jews
> Caucasians
> Malay
> Chickasaw

Rivers:

> the Red River
> the Wabash River
>   (*but*—There are many large rivers in this
>   country.)

Sports stadia and teams:

> Madison Square Garden
> the Cotton Bowl
> the Dodgers and the Yankees

IX
Pronunciation

Many a person speaks far more words than he writes, and a secretary ought to make a favorable impression in conversation. In the following pages the correct pronunciation is shown for a partial list of words often mispronounced due to carelessness or faulty environment. A vowel sound, a consonant sound, or a syllable sound may sometimes be wrongly inserted or omitted or slurred. Sometimes letters that should be silent are sounded and vice versa.

If you decide to perfect your speech you will find yourself observing the speech of others and comparing it with your own. Consult the dictionary whenever you suspect that someone else has made a mistake. This will bring you to a "moment of truth," and you will improve your pronunciation as you enlarge your vocabulary. That is the finest step toward cultivation of improved speech patterns.

ab' ject *(ab' jekt)*
ab' solutely *(ab' so lute li)*
abstemious *(ab stee' mee uss)*
absurd *(ab sserd')*
accede *(ak seed')*
accept *(ak sept')*
accession *(ak sesh' un)*
accessories *(ak sess' o reez)*
accidentally *(ak si den' tal e)*
acclimate *(a kly' mut)*

address (*a dress'*)
admirable (*ad' meer a bl*)
adult (*a dult'*)
aerial (*ay ee' ree al*)
allopathy (*a lopp' a thee*)
ally (*al ly'*—verb; *al' ly*—noun)
apostle (*a poss' ul*)
appendicitis (*ap pen dee sy' tiss*)
applicable (*ap' plick a bl*)
architect (*ar' ki tekt*)
arctic (*ark' tik*)
area (*ay' ree a*)
attacked (*a takt'*)
attitude (*at' i tyud*)
attorney (*a ter' nee*)
autopsy (*aw' top see*)
avenue (*av' a nyu*)
aviation (*ay vi ay' shun*)
battery (*bat' er e*)
being (pronounce the *g*)
beneficent (*be neff' i sent*)
bicycle (*by' syk l*)
biography (*by og' ra fee*)
breadth (*bredth*—pronounce the *d*)
casualty (*cazh' ul tee*)
cemetery (*sem' a ter ree*)
champion (*cham' pee un*)
chasm (*kazm*)
chastisement (*chass tyze' ment*)
chauffeur (*show ferr'*)
chestnut (*chess' nut*)
chocolate (*chock' o lut*)
clique (*kleek*)
comment (*com' ment*)
compromise (*com' pro myze*)
concave (*con cayv'*)
concentrate (*con' sen trayt*)
condolence (*con doe' lens*)
conversant (*con' ver sunt*)
convex (*con vex'*)
corps (*kor*)
creek (*kreek*, not *krik*)
cruel (*kroo' ell*)
data (*day' tah*)
deaf (*deff*)
decade (*deck' ayd*)

decisive *(dee sy' siv)*
defect: verb *(de fekt')*
defect: noun *(de' fekt)*
deficit *(deff' i sitt)*
demonstrable *(de mon' stra bl)*
depot *(dee' po)*
depths (pronounce the *th*)
despicable *(dess' pik a bl)*
dessert *(de zert')*
detour *(dee' toor)*
diamond *(dy' a mund)*
dirigible *(deer' e ji bl)*
distribute *(diss trib' yute)*
divide *(di vyd')*
doing *(doo' ing*—pronounce the *g*)
drowned *(drownd*—not *drownded)*
duly *(dyu' lee)*
duty *(dyu' tee)*
edition *(ee dish' un)*
educate *(edd' yu kate)*
elm (as written, not *ellum)*
envelop: verb *(en vell' up)*
envelope: noun *(en' va lowp)*
epitome *(ee pitt' o mee)*
equitable *(ek' witt a bl)*
etiquette *(ett' i kett)*
every *(ev' a ree)*
exigency *(eks' i jen see)*
exponent *(eks po' nent)*
extant *(eks' tant)*
extraordinary *(eks tror' di nay ree)*
facts (pronounce the *t*)
family *(famm' a lee)*
fasten *(fass' en)*
favorite *(fay' vo ritt)*
figure *(fig' yur)*
film (as written, not *fillum)*
finance *(fin nanss')*
financial *(fin nan' shul)*
financier *(fin nan seer')*
forehead *(fahr' ed)*
formidable *(for' mi da bl)*
fragmentary *(fragg' men ter e)*
friendship *(frend' shipp*—pronounce the *d*)
genuine *(jenn' yu inn)*
gingham *(ghing' um)*

glisten *(gliss' en)*
gondola *(gonn' do la)*
government *(guvv' ern ment*—pronounce both
  n's)
grievous *(gree' vuss)*
guardian *(gar' dee un)*
hasten *(hayss' en)*
height *(hyt*—does not end in *th)*
heinous *(hay' nuss)*
heroism *(her' o izm)*
Herculean *(herk yu lee' un)*
homeopathy *(ho mee opp' a thee)*
horizon *(ho ryz' un)*
hostile *(hoss' till)*
hundred (as written, not *hunnerd)*
idea *(y dee' a)*
ignoramus *(igg no ray' muss)*
immediate *(im mee' dee ut)*
impious *(im' pee uss)*
impotent *(im' po tent)*
incognito *(inn cog nee' to)*
incomparable *(inn com' pa ra bl)*
indictment *(inn dyt' ment)*
industry *(inn' duss tree)*
inexorable *(inn eks' o ra bl)*
inexplicable *(inn eks' plik a bl)*
infamous *(inn' fa muss)*
inquiry *(inn kwy' ree)*
Iowa *(I' o wah)*
irrevocable *(eer rev' o ka bl)*
Italian *(Itt al' yun)*
italics *(it tal' iks)*
judiciary *(joo dish' a ree)*
just (as written, not *jest)*
knew *(nyu)*
lapel *(la pell')*
large *(larj)*
latent *(lay' tent)*
length (as written, not *lenth)*
library (as written, not *ly' bay ree)*
lieu *(lyu)*
lightning *(lyt' ning*—as distinguished from
  lightening)
long-lived *(long lyvd')*
longevity *(lon jev' i tee)*
lyceum *(ly see' um)*

manufacture *(man yu fakt' yur)*
maturity *(ma tyu' rit tee)*
memorable *(mem' o r bl)*
mischievous *(miss' cha vuss)*
municipal *(myu niss' i pul)*
museum *(myu zee' um)*
new *(nyu)*
oblique *(o bleek')*
office *(off' fiss—not awfuss)*
often *(off' en)*
on (as written, not *awn*)
ordeal *(orr' deel)*
osteopath *(oss' tee o path)*
osteopathy *(oss tee opp' a thee)*
overalls (as written, not *over halls*)
parade *(pa rayd'—not prayd)*
partner (as written, not *pard ner*)
patron *(pay' trun)*
pecan *(pik kann')*
pecuniary *(pee kyu' nee ay ree)*
peremptory *(per emp' to ree)*
piano *(pee ann' o)*
picture *(pik' tyur)*
pique *(peek)*
plumber *(plum' er)*
positively *(poz' it tiv lee)*
possess *(po zess')*
precedence *(press' a denss)*
preface *(preff' uss)*
preferable *(preff' er a bl)*
prescription *(pree scripp' shun)*
presentation *(prez en tay' shun)*
quietus *(kwy ee' tuss)*
radiator *(ray' dee ay tor)*
radio *(ray' dee o)*
rambling (as written, not *ram bol ing*)
realm (as written, not *rellum*)
recognize *(rek' og nyz)*
recourse *(ree' corss)*
refutable *(re fyut' a bl)*
reputable *(rep' yut a bl)*
research *(re sertch')*
resources *(ree' sorss ez)*
respite *(res' pit)*
revocable *(rev' o ka bl)*
romance *(ro manss')*

Roosevelt *(Ro' za velt)*
route *(root)*
sagacious *(sa gay' shuss)*
schism *(sizm)*
simultaneous *(sy mull tay' nee uss)*
slippery (as written, not *slip ree)*
solace *(soll' uss)*
solder *(sodd' er)*
sphere *(sfeer)*
status *(stay' tuss)*
strictly (as written, not *strickli)*
student *(styu' dent)*
stupid *(styu' pid)*
subpoena *(sup pee' na)*
subtle *(sutt' tl)*
suit *(syut)*
superfluous *(syu per' floo uss)*
surprise *(ser pryz')*
telegrapher *(tell egg' ra fer)*
temperament (as written, not *temperment)*
tenet *(tenn' ett)*
theater *(thee' a ter)*
tract (as written, not *track)*
trembling (as written, not *trem bol ing)*
tremendous *(tre men' duss)*
tribune *(trib' yun)*
Tuesday *(tyuz' day)*
tube *(tyub)*
tumult *(tyu' mult)*
umbrella (as written, not *um ba rellah)*
usurp *(yu serp')*
Utica *(yu' tik a)*
vagary *(va gay' ree)*
vaudeville *(vaugh' de vil)*
vehement *(vee' a ment)*
vehicle *(vee' hick l)*
verbose *(verbowss')*
victuals *(vitt' ulz)*
was *(wahz)*
water *(wah' ter)*
worsted *(woos' ted)*
what (as written, not *wot)*
wheel (as written, not *weel)*
whether *(hweth' er)*
white *(hwyt)*
wrestle *(ress' l)*

X

Punctuation

If a mark of punctuation does not clarify the text it should be omitted, but the secretary must suit her employer's preference if he instructs her to insert more commas and semicolons than today's magazines and newspapers use. When public changes occur, not every individual immediately approves. Nevertheless, there are certain formalities that must still be observed.

The Apostrophe

As a mark of omission the apostrophe may denote that a word has been contracted intentionally:

> It's time to go.
> Don't go there.

It stands as a mark of possession, after a singular noun and followed by an *s*, or alone after a noun or proper name ending in *s* or *z* or *x* (one-syllable proper names often use an apostrophe followed by an *s*, no matter what letter they end in):

the city's founder
Miss Jones' dress
Mr. Cox' book

It is used alone after plural nouns ending in *s*:

fifteen years' service
the books' titles

Plural nouns not ending in *s* form the possessive by adding an apostrophe and an *s*:

men's clubs
sheep's clothing

The plural of compound nouns and joint possessive nouns is formed by adding an apostrophe followed by an *s* to the second word only:

the Secretary-Treasurer's decision
Mary and John's report cards

No apostrophe is used with possessive pronouns:

his
hers
its
yours
ours
theirs

The apostrophe is used to express duration of time when a plural term is used:

five days' traveling time
twelve months' duration

The Colon

The colon follows an expression introducing a tabulation or a long quotation:

During your first year, you will study such subjects as these: algebra, physics, chemistry, and psychology.

The following quotation is from the *Detroit Free Press:* "Regardless of what may be accomplished, the company will still be involved."

The colon is used to stress a word, phrase, or clause that follows it:

The newspaper published a startling statement: the city had been completely destroyed by fire.

The colon follows a salutation in a letter:

Dear Mr. Watson:
Gentlemen:

The colon is used to separate hours and minutes in expressions of time:

4:15 A.M. CST

The colon is used to separate a title from a subtitle:

Gone with the Wind: A Story of the Old South

The Comma

The presence of a comma, or its absence, can cause different interpretations of a written statement. It is thus of vast importance, particularly in legal documents. (In Carmel, California, the voters approved a plan to use Sunset School "for municipal civic and cultural purposes," but because no comma had been inserted after the word "municipal" the city council argued that they were not empowered to move the City Hall offices to the premises.)

A comma is used between the clauses of a compound sentence if the second clause has its own subject:

John went to the theater, but he left before the play ended.
John went to the theater but left before the play ended.

An adverbial clause usually follows the independent clause, and no comma is used. But for emphasis, it is sometimes placed before the independent clause and is said to be *transposed*. In this transposed position, an adverbial clause is followed by a comma.

Usual order:
John was met by a large delegation when he came home.

Transposed:
When John came home, he was met by a large delegation.

A comma is used in writing large numbers, separating the thousand digits from the million digits, etc.

1,345,000   249,586

Words such as *yes, no,* and *well* are set off by a comma when they occur alone at the beginning of a sentence:

Yes, I will go.
No, I cannot go.
Well, perhaps he is right.

Mild exclamations at the beginning of a sentence can be set off by a comma:

Ah, he might have come after all.

A comma may be used for clarity:

The lion, not the tiger, growled.

Nonrestrictive phrases or clauses (that is, phrases or clauses which could be omitted without affecting the meaning of the main clause) should be set off from the rest of the sentence by a comma or by parenthetical commas:

Mary Brown, who lives next door, is in the third grade.
But   That is the girl who lives next door.

In the same way, commas are used to set off parenthetical expressions:

John, my favorite friend, is visiting me.
That car is, I believe, a new model.

Adjectives in a series of the same rank, modifying the same

noun, are separated by commas unless they are joined by conjunctions:

> We swam in cool, clear, fresh water.
> *But* Cool and clear fresh water was tumbling down the rock cliff.

Commas are used to separate the words of a series:

> The workers picked cherries, peaches, apricots, and plums.
> These delegates to the convention came from New York, Detroit, and Chicago. (Some editors, however, prefer to omit the comma before the *and* in such sentences.)

When a term consisting of years, months, and days is given as a single unit of time, no commas are used:

> Interest will be computed for 6 years 3 months and 2 days.

A comma is used to separate a quotation from the main sentence:

> "Please go with me," the boy said.
> The little girl said, "There is a rabbit."
> "What do you think," Mr. Bleeker asked, "the Mayor will do next?"

The comma also separates the name of the one addressed from the remainder of the sentence:

> Will you come with me, John?
> But, Jane, how do you know that the train is late?
> Gentlemen, we await your decision.
> Mr. Jones, we hope you will come to see us.

A comma is used to set off a sharp expression from the rest of the sentence:

> Don't forget, be here early.
> Wait, I'll go with you.
> Remember, she is leaving tomorrow.

A comma is used to set off an independent expression from the rest of the sentence:

> Naturally, he expected me to be there.
> Obviously, I know what you mean.

> To tell the truth, I really think you should go.
> As a rule, he arrives early.
> Better yet, come an hour earlier.
> Incidentally, what did you think of his speech?

However, a few introductory expressions are more emphatic without punctuation and need not be followed by a comma:

> Doubtless she just couldn't be here.
> At least you tried.
> Of course I will be there.
> Undoubtedly the plane's engines both failed.
> Indeed you may bring your friends with you.

When an adjective follows a noun (its normal order is before the noun), it is set off by commas; when an adjective precedes an article standing directly in front of a noun, a comma follows the adjective:

> The physician, dignified and competent, told them the bad news.
> Dignified and competent, the physician told them the bad news.

When the year follows the month or the month and day, it is set off by a comma:

> He visited me in May, 1963, and stayed three days.
> She left for Europe on June 22, 1967, and returned a month later.

Set off *Incorporated* from the name of a company:

> Johnson Brothers, Incorporated
> General Motors, Incorporated

Set off *Jr.* and *Sr.* from a proper name. A Roman numeral is not set off by a comma. *2d* or *3d* may be set off by a comma, if desired.

> John Murchison, Sr.
> John Murchison, Jr.
> John Murchison III
> John Murchison, 2d or John Murchison 2d
> John Murchison II

Elements of an address are set off by commas:

He lives at 410 South Hawthorne Street, Chicago, Illinois, near the University of Chicago.

She moved here from Los Angeles, California, about two months ago.

A comma is used to set off the transitional adverbs *however* and *moreover* when used within the sentence or as the last word in a sentence:

I will be there, however, as soon as I can.
There is a problem, moreover, which must be solved.
I will be there as soon as I can, however.

Sometimes *though* is used to mean *however*, and should be set off with commas:

I will be there, though, if I can.

No comma is used for prepositional phrases within a sentence unless the phrase comes between the subject and the predicate of the clause:

I am sure that because of your generosity we will be able to build the new dormitory.
The bag, in addition to a hatbox, will be sent to you today.

Set off absolute phrases within a sentence by commas:

The meaning of the letter is emphatic, *you're to carry out the mission without delay,* and should be handled accordingly.

Contrasting expressions within a sentence are set off by commas:

We walk slowly, never fast, to the garage.
She speaks softly, seldom harshly, to her dog.
This letter was meant for you, not for me.
But This letter was meant for you but not for me.

An infinitive phrase used independently is set off by commas, although as a modifier it is not punctuated:

The color is too dark, to list one fault.
The piano is too large to fit in the room.

A confirming question within a sentence is set off by commas:

> He left, did he not, on the noon plane?
> You will go, won't you, to the meeting?

A comma is used to separate a name and a title:

> The letter was from Mr. Jones, our President, and contained a list of instructions for us to follow.
> John Smith, Director of Public Relations, came by to see me.

A comma is used for clarity and to avoid confusion:

> Whoever goes, goes without my consent.
> Whatever occurs, occurs for a reason.

When words are omitted in one part of a sentence because they were used in another part, a comma is used to show where the words were omitted.

> John's telephone number is Main 2-1702, and mine, Main 2-1989.
> On Tuesday we arrive at nine, and on Wednesday, eleven.

A comma is used to separate two or more unrelated numbers:

> On August 1, 1967, 328 people visited the museum.
> Out of eighty, twenty were discarded.

The Dash

The dash (in typing, indicated by two hyphens) is used to introduce an added thought:

> I shall go with you—you don't mind, do you?

and to break the continuity of a thought:

> *The Scherzo Sonata* by Tolstoi is a sad story—but the writing is magnificent.

It is sometimes used before and after a parenthetical expression:

> Henry Higgins—bareheaded and without a coat—left the house and ran down the road.

Quotation Marks

Quotation marks are used to set off any material quoted within a sentence or paragraph. If the quoted material consists of several paragraphs, the opening quotation mark is used at the beginning of the quotation and at the beginning of each paragraph within the quotation; a closing quotation mark, however, is used only at the conclusion of the quotation, not at the end of each paragraph within the quotation, as many untutored persons seem to think.

> The passage he read aloud was from the first chapter:
> "The discovery of this energy brings to us the problem of how to allow it to be used.
> "The use of atomic power throws us back to the Greek legend of Prometheus and the age-old question of whether force should be exerted against law.
> "The man of today must decide whether he will use this power for destruction or for peaceful purposes."
> When he had finished the reading there was loud applause.

Single quotation marks indicate a quotation within a quotation:

> He said, "Did you hear John make the statement, 'I will not go with her,' or were you not present at the time he spoke?"

In printed text, the titles of essays, articles, poems, stories, or chapters are set off within quotation marks, while titles of plays, books, and periodical publications are italicized:

> The name of the article was "I Believe."
> The title of the book was *Journey into Night.*
> It was first published in *Harper's Magazine.*

The Semicolon

A semicolon is used when the conjunction is omitted between parts of a compound sentence:

> I went with them; I should have stayed at home.

It precedes words such as *however, moreover,* or *otherwise* when they introduce the second of two connected full sentences:

> She is arriving at noon; however, she will not stay long.

If parts of a series contain inner punctuation such as a comma, the parts are separated by a semicolon:

> He came to see his mother, who was ill; his sister, who
> lived in the next village; and his old schoolmate.

The Period

A period is used at the end of a sentence to denote a full pause:

> I am going to town. You may go with me if you wish.

It is also used in decimals to separate a whole number from a decimal fraction:

> 5.6%
> $19.20

and following abbreviations:

> Mrs.
> Ph.D.
> etc.

The Ellipsis

To show omission of words in quoted material, three periods are used within a sentence, four at the end:

"Five hundred firemen . . . attended the ball. . . ."
Mr. Brown went on to say: "The shoe department functions smoothly . . . many salespeople have won prizes for efficiency. . . ."

The ellipsis may also be used to mark a thought expressed hesitantly:

He said, "If . . . if I do go with you, will you return early?"

The Question Mark

A question mark closes a question:

What time is it?

A question mark is used to express a doubt:

He is older (?) than she.

If the question is indirect, no question mark is used:

I wonder whether he will be here.

When a question is asked in the middle of a sentence, a question mark is used:

They are arriving, aren't they, on the noon train?

When a question is enclosed in parentheses, the question mark is inside the parentheses, not at the end of the sentence:

The magazine (did you see it?) describes the city in detail.

If the question mark is part of a quotation, it is placed *inside* the closing quotation mark; if it is not a part of the quotation, it is placed *outside* the closing quotation mark:

> The statement ended, "And is that all?"
> What did he mean by "jobless years"?

If the last word in a sentence is an abbreviation and thus contains a period, the question mark is also used:

> Do you think he will arrive by 4:00 P.M.?

When it is desired to make a question of a statement, the question mark is used:

> She is really going?
> He is arriving today?
> Really?

The Exclamation Point

An exclamation point is used when making extravagant claims:

> Here is the finest sweeper on the market!

or to express deep feeling:

> The announcement was unbelievable!

or after a word or phrase charged with emotion:

> Quick! We don't want to be late.

or for double emphasis:

> Did you catch that innuendo!

Parentheses

Parentheses are used to enclose matter that is introduced by way of explanation:

If the lessor (the person owning the property) agrees to allow the lessee (the person renting the property) to have a dog on the premises, it is permissible.

or to enclose figures used to enumerate items:

The book included chapters on (a) capitalization, (b) spelling rules, (c) troublesome verbs, and (d) punctuation.

or to enclose citations of authority:

The definition of *action* is "process or state of being active." (Webster)

or to enclose figures repeated for the sake of clarity, as in legal documents:

He was willed five thousand dollars ($5,000) by his uncle. You will be paid twenty (20) percent interest.

Italics

Italics are sometimes used for emphasis:

Notice where you *are*, not where you *have been*.

But the best writing avoids italics for this purpose, depending on choice of language to bring out the emphasis:

Rather notice where you are now than ruminate about where you have been previously.

As mentioned earlier, italics are used for the names of books, pamphlets, and periodicals:

Saturday Evening Post
Black Beauty
Washington Daily News

The names of ships are also italicized:

The Sea Witch
The U.S.S. *Heinz*

When typing, indicate italics by underlining.

XI
Numerals

In printed text, a number used for quick reference or for comparison with other numbers in the same section should be in numerical form:

> An excavation of 500 feet can be finished as rapidly as 200 feet if the right equipment is available.

Numbers under 100 are spelled out in the average prose text. In legal documents numbers are written in both words and figures to prevent misunderstanding, and the same is true in papers that transfer land title:

> The west thirty (30) feet of Lot Nine (9) in Block Four (4) . . .

Approximate round numbers are spelled out:

> The station is about fifty blocks away.
> He found nearly two hundred dollars.

Two sets of numbers occurring in a sentence are differentiated by alternate spelling and figures:

> Three of the men drove 2,000 miles each; four drove 3,000 miles each; and only one drove the complete 5,000 miles.

At the beginning of a sentence, if the word designating a number is a simple one- or two-word expression, it should be spelled out; otherwise it is given in numerals:

Sixteen new cars were delivered.
Thirty or forty bushels were needed.
2,746,892 copies were purchased.

Dollars and Cents

When the amount of dollars given is not followed by cents, omit the decimal point and ciphers:

$3
$1200
but $17.75

Use the dollar sign before the number rather than the word *dollar* or *dollars* after the number:

He gave the boy a $5 bill.
The house rents for $100 a month;
but The budget called for $116 million.

Repeat the dollar sign with successive numbers:

In his pocket the police found several $10, $20, and $100 bills.

A series of prices is written in figures only:

There were dresses priced at $12, $18, and $25.

The dollar sign is not used when the figure given is in cents alone, except in statistical work when the part of the dollar is carried out to more than two decimal places:

$0.3564

Use the cent sign (¢) after amounts less than one dollar but never with a decimal point:

25¢
not .25¢—for that would mean one-fourth of a cent.

Time

When a figure and a word come together expressing time, connect the two with a hyphen:

> a 24-hour day
> > *but* a day of 24 hours
>
> an 8-year guarantee
> > *but* a guarantee of eight years
>
> two 2-year 5% notes
> > *but* two notes for two years at 5%

Hours and minutes and seconds are separated by a colon:

> 10:05:02 A.M.

Never use *this* A.M. instead of *this morning*. With A.M. or P.M. the word *o'clock* should not be used:

> I will meet you at 4 P.M.
> I will meet you at four o'clock this afternoon.

Ciphers after the number of the hour are not necessary. For exact *noon* and *midnight* it is correct to use the words:

> I will meet you at 12 noon.
> The horn blew at 12 midnight.

Separating Digits

All numbers above 9999 are written with commas:

> 10,000
> 2,436,936

Numbers below 10,000 are usually written without commas, but commas may be used if they help in the reading of the numbers:

2,400
4,860
9,500

Patent numbers are written with commas:

Patent No. 3,436,987

But serial numbers are written without commas:

Motor Number 2458765
Policy Number 894325

Omit commas in large fractions and decimals, page numbers, street or house numbers, telephone numbers, year numbers, room numbers, form numbers, and list numbers:

Page 3486
Murray Hill 8–9971
Room 2630
Form 2317–A

Dates

The day is written in numerals without *th*, *st*, *nd*, or *d*, unless the day is written before the name of the month:

May 1, 1969
In the August 21 edition
On the 2nd of June, 1970

In legal documents dates are spelled out:

the twelfth day of August, A.D. Nineteen Hundred and Sixty-Nine

Hyphen

Written-out numbers below one hundred are hyphenated:

> thirty-three
> twenty-eight
> ninety-nine

but hundreds and thousands are not hyphenated:

> six hundred thousand
> three hundred million

When modifying a noun, numbers are hyphenated, as are any compound adjectives:

> a five-thousand-foot mountain
> a three-foot rule

Fractions of one are hyphenated:

> one-third
> one-fifth
>   *but* one twenty-third
> three-quarters

Do not write one part of the fraction as a numeral and the other as a word:

> one-fourth-inch bolt *but* ¼" bolt
> seven-eighths of a yard

When one plus a fraction is used, the noun is plural and the verb singular:

> 1-5/8 inches is needed.
> 2-3/4 miles is the length of the track.

Figures

As a general rule, write out numbers up to and including one hundred, and use figures for numbers over one hundred. If a number can be written as one or two words, even though it is over one hundred, do so: *four hundred, five million, two thousand*

Use the short form for writing numbers over a thousand not pertaining to money:

fourteen hundred, not *one thousand four hundred*

Use figures for money:

1 cent, 5 cents, 20,000 dollars or 1¢, 5¢, $20,000

Amounts of money are written out when beginning a sentence:

One cent was contributed by each child.
not 1¢ was contributed. . . .
Fifty thousand dollars was the grand prize.
not $50,000 was the grand prize.

The dollar sign is repeated in a series unless in tabulated form:

The bonds could be purchased in denominations of $10,000, $12,000, $15,000, and $20,000.
The bonds could be purchased in denominations of the following amounts:

$10,000
12,000
15,000
20,000

No decimal point and ciphers are used with even amounts of money unless in tabulated form. If tabulated, and some amounts contain cents and some do not, the even amounts should contain ciphers:

$55, $19, $5,000, $13,500
not $55.00, $19,00, $5,000.00, $13,500.00

When tabulated:

$19.36
5.00
2.14
37.00
1.23
.19
.02

The form *10 cents,* not *$.10,* should be used in a sentence unless it is used in relation to other amounts of money in which a dollar sign has been used:

The price of the candy is 10 cents.
>   *but*   The fee of $85.50 included the $.50 tax charge.

If the sentence cannot be written more gracefully, use a comma or dash to separate the numbers or else spell out one of them:

> During the year 1965, 16 million people visited the park.
> In 1965, there were 16 million people visiting the park.
> We received 1,213—113 of which were of inferior quality.
> Of the 1,213 that we received, 113 were of inferior quality.

Use the general rule in giving the age of a person or a period of time (write out up to and including one hundred; use figures over one hundred):

> She is twelve years old.
> He has held the same position for twenty-six years.
> She is now 105 years of age.
> The company has been in the same building for 102 years.

In compound adjectives denoting age, the words designating time may be used before *old*, but in that event the words *year* and *day* must appear in the singular:

> a 12-weeks-old baby elephant
> a 6-months-old pony
> a 200-year-old building
> a 3-day-old kitten

When a decimal occurs with no unit before it, use a cipher for quick interpretation:

> a 0.75-yard measurement
> rainfall of 0.356 inches

Dimensions

The signs reserved for technical writing are ′ for feet, ″ for inches, and *x* for *by*:

9' x 12'
8" x 10"

Ciphers can be used to indicate exact measurement if they improve clarity:

9'0" x 12'0" x 20'6"

Weights and Measures

Abbreviations are used without capitalization:

6 lbs. 3 oz.
192 bbls.
or
6 pounds 3 ounces
192 barrels

In a compound adjective showing a weight or a measure, the numeral is hyphenated to a singular noun:

600-mile-an-hour speed
    but speed of 600 miles an hour
a 40-hour week
    but a week of 40 hours

Percentages

The numeral is retained whether or not a percent sign is used:

a 5% price reduction
a loss of 10 percent
almost 30 percent of the population

For percentages in succession use the sign after each numeral:

30% to 50%
6%, 8%, and 10%

Page-Numbering

On legal documents a page number is centered at the bottom of each page; on other papers it is usually shown at the top of the page. Manuscripts and briefs are numbered in the upper right corner, while papers that are to be bound at the left are numbered in the lower right corner. Title pages are not numbered. A first page of a work or of a chapter is not marked with the number, although the numbering of the following pages takes into consideration the normal number of the first page.

Write all numbers at exactly the same place on each page of a given work by determining the place on the typewriter scale to be matched for each page.

It is acceptable to use a short dash before and after the page number: -3-, without a period. Never use quotation marks and never type the word *page* before the number. Frequently the number stands alone: 2, without a period.

Abbreviation or Sign for "No."

These are usually omitted:

> Building 38
>   *not* Building No. 38
> Invoice 3457
>   *not* Invoice #3457
> Page 92
>   *not* Page No. 92

In text, however, it may be convenient to use the abbreviation:

> When he came to No. 16 he halted.
> The only houses to be painted this year are Nos. 16, 17, and 18.

Plural

Form the plural of a numeral or other character by adding *s* or *es* or *'s*. If the number is spelled out, use the *s* or *es*, not *'s*:

> 5s and 6s *or* 5's and 6's
> fives and sixes
> the 1890s *or* the 1890's
> DC-8Bs *or* DC-8B's

Ordinals

Ordinals up to *one hundredth* are spelled out in printed text:

> the fourth race
> the seventh and eighth floors
> Second Street
> the Twenty-Sixth Legislature

Often the more graceful form is used, for language is a tool and discretion will often dictate variations not in a book of rules.

Large Numbers

If a figure or the word *several* precedes *hundred, thousand, million, billion*, etc., the singular form is used. After *many* the plural form is used:

> six hundred pages
> many hundreds of pages
> six million years
> several million years
> population of ten million

Roman Numerals

Arabic	Roman		Arabic	Roman
1	I		40	XL
2	II		50	L
3	III		60	LX
4	IV		70	LXX
5	V		80	LXXX
6	VI		90	XC
7	VII		100	C
8	VIII		150	CL
9	IX		200	CC
10	X		300	CCC
11	XI		400	CD
12	XII		500	D
13	XIII		600	DC
14	XIV		700	DCC
15	XV		800	DCCC
16	XVI		900	CM
17	XVII		1000	M
18	XVIII		1500	MD
19	XIX		2000	MM
20	XX		3000	MMM
30	XXX		4000	MMMM

A dash *over* a Roman numeral
multiplies it by 1000:

5000	$\overline{V}$
6000	$\overline{VI}$
100,000	$\overline{C}$
1,000,000	$\overline{M}$

Dates:

1900	MCM
1910	MCMX
1920	MCMXX
1930	MCMXXX
1940	MCMXL
1950	MCML
1955	MCMLV
1960	MCMLX
1970	MCMLXX
1980	MCMLXXX

XII
Legal Documents

When a secretary is expecting to be called on to take legal dictation, she ought to enroll in a refresher course in special terminology, because a knowledge of legal grammalogues is a great convenience. A grammalogue is a shorthand shortcut for full expressions often used, and when taking dictation it is of immense comfort to be able to write in one stroke the representation for "time is of the essence" or other phrases of equal length—"writ of habeas corpus" or "denied certiorari," for instance. She can have her notes complete before the dictator has finished his sentence because she knows what he means to say and how to record it quickly.

When you are asked to type a legal document, use plain white legal paper 8½″ x 13″ or legal cap paper of the same size having a wide ruled margin at the left and a narrow ruled margin at the right. The typing must be kept within these ruled lines. Briefs are written on paper 8″ x 10½″ with ruled margins. Wills are written on heavy noncorrasable paper of legal size without ruled margins.

Always double-space papers and reports, with triple spaces between paragraphs. Retain a two-inch margin at the top and a one-inch margin at the bottom of the page. If plain paper is used rather than ruled, leave a 1½″ margin on the left and a ¾″ margin on the right.

Indent paragraphs ten spaces, and for land descriptions or quotations that are single-spaced, indent an additional five spaces.

Carbon copies to be signed (called *duplicate originals*) are typed on the same kind of paper as the original. Carbon copies not to be signed are made on legal-size onionskin paper.

Number the pages in the center of the bottom of the page (¾" from the bottom edge), except for briefs that are numbered in the upper right corner, the first page number not marked.

If an error is made in typing a legal document, retype the entire page, because erasures may cause a court contest at a later date. Erasures are never allowed, especially in wills.

Legal documents are bound with a sheet of heavy backing paper (9" x 15"). The backing sheet should be folded to provide four sections of the sheet 9" long. On one of these sections type an endorsement and label briefly to describe what the document represents. Following is an example of an endorsed mortgage backing:

> No. A-31075
> RELEASE OF OIL AND GAS LEASE
> FROM
> WILLIAM P. ALLEN
> TO
> FIRST NATIONAL BANK AND TRUST CO.

Printed legal forms of many kinds, referred to as "law blanks," are obtainable at stationery stores. They are easily filled in on the typewriter and are quickly read. They may sometimes serve as a guide in drafting a document.

When writing numbers in legal documents, write them in words and repeat them immediately in numerals inside parentheses:

> ten thousand five hundred and seventy-five (10,575) dollars

or

> ten thousand five hundred and seventy-five dollars ($10,575).

Dates may be spelled out or may express the day and the year in numerals, with the month always spelled out.

The following words and phrases often used in legal documents are customarily written in full capitals, usually followed by a comma, a colon, or no punctuation:

THIS AGREEMENT, made this second day of . . .
KNOW ALL MEN BY THESE PRESENTS, that . . .
IN WITNESS WHEREOF I have this day . . .
MEMORANDUM OF AGREEMENT made this twenty-
fifth day of . . .

Case Titles

Case titles are always underscored, followed by a comma,
the volume and page numbers, and date:

Johnson v. Smith, 201 Okla. 433, 32 Am. Rep. 168 (1901)

Notary Public Forms

The following are commonly used forms of notary public
acknowledgments on legal documents:

1. For an individual:
   State of _____) SS
   County of_____)
   On the _____ day of _____, 19____, before
   me came _____, known to me to be the
   individual described in and who executed the foregoing in-
   strument and acknowledged that he executed the same.
   (S)_____
   Notary Public
   (Stamp and Seal)
   (The stamp is not required in every state.)

2. For a corporation:
   State of _____) SS
   County of _____)
   On the _____ day of _____, 19____, before
   me personally appeared _____, to me
   known, who, being by me duly sworn, did depose and say
   that he resides at _____;
   that he is _____ (title) of _____
   _____ (Company), the
   corporation described in and which executed the foregoing

instrument; that he knows the seal of said corporation; that the seal affixed to said instrument is such corporate seal; that it was so affixed by order of the _____ _____ (title) of said corporation; and that he signed his name thereto by like order.

                              (S)_____
                                  Notary Public

(Seal)

3. For a partnership:
   State of _____) SS
   County of _____)
      On this _____ day of _____, 19_____, before me personally appeared _____, to me known and known to me to be a member of_____ _____ (name of partnership), and the person described in and who executed the foregoing instrument in the firm name of _____, and he duly acknowledged to me that he executed the same as and for the act and deed of said firm of _____ _____.

                              (S)_____
                                  Notary Public in and for the
                                  above named state and county.

(Seal)

Codicils to a Will

Additions to and changes in a will are made by an instrument known as a codicil, sometimes written on the last page of the will. It must be dated, formally executed, signed, witnessed, and probated with the will. Here is a *sample of a codicil to last will and testament:*

   I, JOHN ROE MOORE, a resident of the City of Chicago, County of Cook, State of Illinois, do hereby make, publish, and declare the following as and for a codicil to the Will and Testament heretofore by me executed, bearing date of the _____th day of _____, 19_____.
      FIRST: (state provisions)
      SECOND: (state provisions)
      In all other respects and except as hereinbefore set forth,

I hereby republish, ratify, and confirm my said Will, dated
the _____th day of _____, _____.
    WITNESS MY HAND AND SEAL this _____ day
of _____, 19_____.
               (S)_____
                                  (SEAL)

Sample of Attestation:

The foregoing Codicil, consisting of one-half page, containing no interlineations or erasures, was on the date
thereof signed by the above-named Testator and at the same
time published and declared by him to be a Codicil to his
Last Will and Testament. The said Testator signed this
instrument in the presence of the undersigned, who acted as
attesting witnesses at his request. Each of the undersigned
signed as a witness in the presence of the Testator and in
the presence of each other. At the time of the execution of
this Codicil the said Testator was of sound mind and
memory and under no undue influence or restraint.
NAME: ADDRESS:
(S)_____   _____
(S)_____   _____

The secretary usually types the name and address of each
witness beneath these lines.

Agreements

Contracts or agreements should state the obligations of
each party as shown in the following sample contract:

THIS AGREEMENT, made this _____ day of
_____, 19_____, between _____
_____ of _____,
_____, First Party (hereinafter
called the Seller), and _____,
a corporation incorporated under the laws of the State of
_____, with principal place of
business in _____, _____, Second
Party (hereinafter called the Purchaser),

W I T N E S S E T H :

WHEREAS the Seller has this day agreed to _____

_____; and

WHEREAS the Purchaser is willing to _____

_____; and

WHEREAS _____;

NOW, THEREFORE, it is agreed that _____

_____.

WITNESS the signatures of the parties hereto on the date aforesaid.

(S)_____
Seller

(S)_____
Purchaser
by _____
President

(CORPORATE SEAL)

Proxy

A proxy is a form of power of attorney given by one person to another, authorizing the second person to vote in lieu of the first person at a meeting of a corporation. Following is a sample proxy:

(CORPORATE SEAL)

I, JOHN WILLIAM BROWN, do hereby constitute and appoint PHILIP RAYMOND JOHNSON attorney and agent for me, to vote as my proxy at a meeting of the stockholders of JOHN A. BROWN COMPANY, according to the number of votes I should be entitled to cast if personally present.

DATE:_____

(S)_____

Legal Terms

Here is a partial list of legal terms that the secretary may have occasion to use:

abstract of title A brief history of the title to a piece of real estate, including data regarding transfer of the property from the time of the first recorded owner to the present owner.

accessory after the fact A person who aids one whom he knows to be a felon.

accessory before the fact A person who instigates or contributes to the commission of a crime but who does not actually take part in it.

acknowledgment A certification appearing at the end of a legal paper showing that the paper was duly acknowledged and executed.

administrator (male) or *administratrix* (female) One appointed by the Court to administer an estate.

affidavit A certification attesting the authenticity of statements made in a legal paper.

assessment A levy made on property for improvements.

advocate A person who pleads the cause of another before a tribunal or judicial court.

answer A statement made by the defendant through his attorney stating his version of the situation (often called a plea).

appeal The act of taking a legal case to a higher court.

appurtenances, tenements, and hereditaments
Appurtenances are improvements that pertain to the land; *tenements* are rights and interests that pertain to the land; and *hereditaments* are rights and property inherited or inheritable.

arraignment The calling of an accused person into court, reading the indictment to him, and asking him whether he is guilty or not guilty.

attachment A court order authorizing a seizure or a taking into custody of property or monies to satisfy a claim.

attestation A certification as to the genuineness of a copy.

attorney One who is legally appointed by another to transact business for him.

attorney-in-fact One who is appointed by another, by means of a letter or a power of attorney, to transact business for him out of court.

bequeath To make a bequest or to give personal property by will.

beneficiary The person who is benefited by a gift, proceeds of an insurance policy, income from a trust estate, etc.

brief The written argument of an attorney supporting his contention as to the correct interpretation of the law and the proper inference from the evidence in a particular case.

burden of proof A term meaning that the party making a claim must prove it. Burden of proof rests on the plaintiff.

capital punishment The death penalty.

corporal punishment Punishment applied to the body of the offender.

certified copy A copy of an instrument made from the records in a Recorder's office and certified to by the Recorder as being an exact copy of the paper on file or of record.

certiorari A writ from a superior court to call up for review the records of an inferior court.

change of venue A change in the place of trial.

civil action An action to enforce a civil right or to remedy a private wrong.

complaint A formal allegation against a party.

conditional sale A contract covering goods sold and delivered to a buyer on condition that he make periodic payments thereon (or meet other stipulated conditions).

criminal action An action in which it is sought to determine the guilt of a person who is accused of a crime specifically prohibited by law.

cross-complaint A complaint seeking affirmative relief against a codefendant.

defalcation A misappropriation of funds by one who has them in trust.

demurrer A plea by the defendant asking the court to dismiss the action because of insufficient cause for complaint.

deposition A testimony under oath in writing, often taken orally and signed after it has been recorded.

easement An acquiring privilege or right of use or enjoyment which one person may have in the land of another.

eminent domain That superior dominion of the sovereign power over property which authorizes the state to appropriate all or any part of it to a necessary public use, reasonable compensation being awarded.

encumbrance A claim or lien upon an estate.

escrow A deed, bond, or other written engagement delivered to a third person to be delivered by him to the grantee upon performance of some condition.

felony Any of various crimes graver in their penal consequences than those called misdemeanors.

fiduciary Held in trust; confidential; one who holds in trust for another.

foreclosure suit A suit brought to foreclose a mortgage.

garnishment Legal notice to one to appear in court, usually regarding the attachment of property to secure a debt.

grand jury An appointed group of citizens to examine accusations against persons charged with crime and to issue bills of indictment if the evidence warrants.

habeas corpus A common-law writ to bring a party before a court or judge, usually when the party is confined in jail.

holographic will A will entirely written, dated, and signed in the handwriting of the maker.

impeachment Arraignment of a public officer for misconduct while in office.

indictment The formal written statement charging one or more persons with an offense, as framed by the prosecuting authority of the state and issued by the Grand Jury.

injunction A court writ requiring a party to perform or to forbear certain acts.

interlocutory Intermediate; not final or definite.

intestate A person who dies without having made a will.

judgment The decree or sentence of a court.

jurisdiction The legal power, right, or authority to hear and determine a cause or causes.

larceny The unlawful taking of objects with intent to deprive the rightful owner.

legatee One to whom a legacy is bequeathed.

letters of administration The instrument by which an administrator or administratrix is authorized to administer the estate of a deceased person.

letters patent An instrument covering rights and title to an invention or public lands.

letters testamentary An instrument authorizing an executor of a will to act.

libel Written public defamation.

malfeasance The performing of an act which a person ought not to perform.

mandamus A writ issued by a superior court directing some inferior court or person in authority to perform some specific duty.

misdemeanor A crime less than a felony.

misfeasance A trespass or injurious act.

mortgage A written conveyance of property intended to be a security for the payment of money.

motion An application made to a court to obtain an order, ruling, or direction.

Notary Public A public officer who attests or certifies deeds, affidavits, and depositions.

perjury False swearing; voluntary violation of an oath.

petit jury A body of twelve persons selected impartially to hear cases and render decisions under the direction of a judge.

plea An allegation of fact as distinguished from a demurrer; in common law practice a defendant's answer to the plaintiff's declaration or, in criminal practice, the accused person's answer to the charge against him.

probate Official proof, especially of an instrument offered as the last will and testament of a person deceased.

proxy Written power to act for another in a specific instance.

quiet title suit Proceedings brought to perfect the title to property.

retaining order A court order temporarily restraining a party from committing a certain act until the court can decide on whether or not an injunction should be issued.

slander A false report maliciously uttered and tending to injure the reputation of another.

statute of limitations A statute assigning a certain time after which rights cannot be enforced by legal action.

stay of execution Court order to withhold execution of a judgment.

subpoena A writ commanding the addressee to attend court.

subpoena duces tecum A subpoena which orders a witness to bring certain documents into court.

summons A warning or citation to appear in court.

testator (m.) or *testatrix* (f.) A person who leaves a will in force at death.

trust An equitable right or interest in property distinct from the legal ownership.

usury Interest in excess of the legal rate charged to a borrower for the use of money.

verdict The decision of a jury on the matter submitted in trial.

vested rights Rights that are permanent and undisputed.

waiver Act of intentionally abandoning some known right, claim, or privilege. Also, the instrument evidencing such an act.

without prejudice Without effect upon any rights that existed previously.

writ An order issued by a court commanding the performance or nonperformance of some act.

XIII
The Accounts

The one subject about which the average secretary is more negligent than she should be is bookkeeping. It is true that this is a field requiring special training, but the secretary in a modern office ought to know its simple mechanics.

Property Rights

Property owned by a business organization and used in its operation is known as *assets*. The interest of the proprietor in the assets of the business is called his *proprietorship*, *net worth*, or *capital*. If the business is free of claims against these assets except for those of the proprietor, then *assets equal proprietorship*. If John Brown purchased a dry-cleaning business for $10,000, his financial condition would be expressed in this way: Assets $10,000 equal proprietorship $10,000.

Additional property can be obtained either by borrowing money and using the money to purchase the property needed, or by purchasing the property with a promise to pay for it at some future date.

Those from whom businessmen borrow on account are known as *creditors*. The creditor has a claim on the property until the proprietor pays him in accordance with agreement. This claim is known as the *liabilities* of the business.

For example, John Brown borrows $5,000 from a bank to use in the operation of his dry-cleaning establishment. The bank thus becomes his creditor. This $5,000 increase in Brown's assets is accompanied by a corresponding claim on his assets which the bank possesses until the borrowed $5,000 is repaid. If Brown purchases equipment and merchandise from the American Dry Cleaning Equipment Company amounting to $5,000 and promises to pay for it in five years, the American Dry Cleaning Equipment Company becomes another creditor. If he fails to pay the $5,000 the company can enforce its claim by legal action, and this claim of the company on Brown's assets is another liability.

Assets of a business are, therefore, subject to two kinds of claim: those arising from the rights of creditors and those arising from the rights of the proprietor. The sum of these rights is equal to the value of the assets. Thus, *assets equal liabilities plus proprietorship*.

Property and property rights are inseparable. The amount of property is exactly equal to the amount of property rights (sometimes called *equities*).

The proprietorship may be one man, two men (in a partnership), half a dozen men, or numerous people operating a corporation.

The proprietor must know the effect of his business transactions on his assets, liabilities, and proprietorship in order to make decisions regarding future operations. Accounts furnish him with a concrete record for this purpose.

If he is considering whether or not to employ additional salesmen, he ought to know the results he is obtaining from his present sales force and be able to decide what results might be obtained by employing additional personnel. If he is considering the purchase of additional merchandise, equipment, or space, he ought to give attention to the results he is getting from his present facilities.

The efficient proprietor is always seeking information concerning the effect of his past operations, in order to plan his future operations. Such plans are known as *budgets*. Therefore the primary purpose of accounting records is to give the proprietor information concerning the nature of his liabilities and proprietorship, as well as to furnish him a concrete record of the effect of the business operations on these.

The purpose of accounting is to (1) record, (2) analyze and classify, and (3) summarize the activities of the business and their effects on each enterprise. Accounting simply reduces to writing the activities of a business.

The Specialized Fields in Accounting

Auditing

Independent accountants examine records and reports and issue a statement of opinion regarding their accuracy, together with a report containing confidential advice to the management.

Budgetary Accounting

This presents in account form the transactions planned for the coming period and summarizes these transactions in accounting statements.

Cost Accounting

This stresses costs of processes and products, particularly manufacturing costs.

Income-Tax Accounting

Reflecting the latest decisions of income-tax authorities, this determines the correct amount of tax liability based on income.

Accounting Statements

Accounting statements (1) list a description of and amounts of property, together with ownership rights, and (2) report the effects of the operations on the owner's equity.

The first is known as the *balance sheet*, showing the assets together with the rights of the creditors and of the proprietor; the second is known as the *income statement*, showing income and costs of operation, with the resulting increase or decrease in proprietorship. The balance sheet shows the financial condition of the business at a given time; the income statement covers the periods between any two balance sheets.

These summaries are interesting to persons other than the proprietors. When the owner of the business wishes to borrow money from a bank, the bank officers, in order to judge his ability to repay the loan, ask for information on the assets and liabilities and the profits earned in previous periods. Creditors request the same information before selling merchandise on account. The Internal Revenue Service also requires a similar statement to be assured that the income tax for the coming year is being estimated properly.

A large business has hundreds and even thousands of assets to list, and the classification commonly used consists of current assets, fixed assets, and deferred charges to expenses.

Current assets appear in the form of cash or items that may reasonably be expected to be converted into cash in the near future by the regular operation of the business. When listed on the balance sheet these assets are arranged in the order in which they will be converted. Columns are also provided to show the quantity, description, price, and extensions. When all these sheets are extended and totaled, their sum is entered on the balance sheet as merchandise inventory.

Fixed assets are those of a permanent nature that will not be converted into cash as long as they serve the needs of the business. They are not intended for resale but are expected to wear out in the operation of the business. They include store equipment, office equipment, delivery equipment, building, land, etc.

Deferred charges to expenses are those assets purchased for use in the business that will be consumed in the near future. They include store supplies, office supplies, and prepaid insurance.

The classification commonly used for liabilities is similar to that for assets: (1) current liabilities, (2) fixed liabilities, and (3) deferred credits to income.

Current liabilities are those that will be due within a short time. For example, if John Brown purchases equipment on account with the agreement that he will pay for it within thirty days, this transaction results in a current liability. The general rule followed is that, if the liability comes due within one year after the balance sheet date, it is a current liability. Under this heading are found notes payable, accounts payable, and accrued liabilities.

Notes payable are promises given by the proprietor to someone to whom he owes money. He may give these to a creditor from whom he has purchased equipment or merchandise, or to a bank when borrowing money.

Accounts payable are the financial obligations of a business, usually arising from a purchase on account, when the buyer has given his promise to pay at some future time for the goods received.

Accrued liabilities are amounts owed to the government on taxes, to employees on wages, or to creditors on interest. If one of these is unusually high, it may be set up singly, under some designation such as "taxes payable."

Fixed liabilities are those that will not be due for a comparatively long time after they are contracted. They usually arise in the purchase of fixed assets and include those liabilities that will not be liquidated within one year from the date of the balance sheet: mortgages payable or bonds payable. A mortgage payable represents a debt owed by a business for which the creditor possesses a mortgage on a particular asset. Bonds payable are long-term obligations of corporations commonly evidenced by bonds, a debt to be paid more than one year hence.

Deferred credits to income is the unearned portion of the payment a business is paid in advance for a service. For example, an insurance company receives in one fiscal period a payment for insurance that extends over a future fiscal period. The unearned portion of the premium is a deferred credit to income and would usually be listed as unearned premium income.

The Balance Sheet

Usually the purpose of any business is to increase its proprietorship—that is, to make money. Accounting records should provide the information that enables a proprietor to know if he is doing so, and it should aid him in accomplishing this. The amount of profit or loss incurred during a given period is the most important single fact.

A balance sheet shows the proprietor the amount of his proprietorship so that he can determine whether his proprietorship is increasing or decreasing, but it does not show him the cause of the increase or decrease.

The Income Statement

At various intervals the proprietor has to plan to increase his profit and eliminate future losses. For this he needs a report that shows him the amount of his sales, the cost of procuring and selling the goods, and the difference, which is the profit or the loss. The income statement gives him such information. The period it covers is known as the fiscal period.

The income statement reports on sales, cost of goods sold, gross profit on sales, operating expenses, and depreciation.

Sales in a mercantile business are the total amount customers have paid or have agreed to pay for merchandise sold them. Other types of business make sales of commodities and services designated by different terms. Railroads have passenger revenue or freight revenue, whereas professional men have fees, and investment trusts have interest income and dividend income. The word *sales,* then, means the gross return from operations.

Cost of goods sold is the purchase price paid by a business for the goods it has sold, as distinguished from the sales price. Cost of goods sold is made up of (1) the price charged by the seller as shown on the invoice of sale; and (2) the freight and drayage charges for the delivery of the goods.

Gross profit on sales is derived by subtracting the cost of merchandise sold from the total sales, representing the profit that would be made if no expenses were incurred in conducting the business. Because expenses are always incurred, they must be considered in determining profit. The difference between the amount received from sales and the cost of the merchandise sold is termed *gross* profit on sales; the expenses of operating the business must be deducted to obtain the *net* profit.

Operating expenses include all commodities and services expended in the operation of a business—services of personnel, paper and twine, electricity, fuel, postage, etc.

Depreciation is the cost arising from the decrease in value of the fixed assets. Not only are supplies and services used to operate a business, but fixed assets—such as office equipment and store equipment—are gradually worn out through use.

The income statement therefore shows the result of the operations of a specific business during a particular period of time. It lists the income from sales and subtracts from this the expenses of the business in making such sales. The last figure is the *net profit* from operations.

The Account

Each time a business performs a transaction, a change is made in one or more elements of the equation *assets equal liabilities plus proprietorship*. Regardless of the number of transactions, the results of all changes must be ascertained in order to prepare an accurate balance sheet and an accurate income statement at the end of the fiscal period. To accomplish this, each transaction must be recorded as it occurs. The *account* is the method used to record these individual transactions, and it is from this word that the subject of accounting receives its name.

The account is the record of each item entered on the balance sheet and on the income statement: the increases and decreases that occur. In its simplest form the account provides (1) the name of the customer, (2) transactions decreasing the amount of proprietorship, and (3) transactions increasing the amount of the same item.

The ledger, which is a group of accounts, contains a page for each account, or several pages if the account is large. A separate account is maintained for each entry on the balance sheet and the income statement. Accounts are arranged in the ledger in the same order in which they are listed on the accounting statements. Current asset accounts precede fixed asset accounts, while all asset accounts come before liability accounts. Proprietorship accounts are listed last. Loose-leaf ledgers should be used, so that new accounts may be inserted alphabetically.

The Trial Balance

If the bookkeeper has correctly recorded each transaction, the total of all the debits in all the accounts will equal the total of the credits in all the accounts. A test is made at intervals, usually at the end of the month, to check whether the debits do equal the credits, and this test is known as a trial balance. This summarizes the ledger information. If the sum of the debits does not equal the sum of the credits, it is evident that an error has been made, and then the bookkeeper has the job of reconciling.

Mixed Accounts

If all transactions recorded in the accounts coincide with the accounting period as shown on the balance sheet and the income statement, the trial balance is a satisfactory check. But it is impossible to arrange transactions so that there will be no carry-overs between accounting periods. A means must therefore be provided to meet this condition, and we have what is called a mixed account. This is an account with a balance that is partly a balance-sheet amount and partly an income-statement amount.

For example, the trial balance amount for the account called Office Supplies summarizes all office supplies purchased plus those on hand at the beginning of the period covered. To find out just how many office supplies have been used during the accounting period, an inventory of office supplies is taken. The office supplies on hand are a balance-sheet entry; the office supplies used are an income-statement entry. Therefore the account Office Supplies is a mixed account.

The adjustment of mixed accounts must deteremine the correct balance-sheet amount and the correct income-statement amount for any trial-balance entry that is mixed. For example, a typewriter is recorded as an asset at the time of purchase and appears in the trial balance. The depreciation of the typewriter is not recorded each day and must instead be recorded by an adjustment at the end of the accounting period.

Other types of business operations continually affect accounts—insurance expires, wages and salaries accrue. It is necessary to record all such mixed accounts. A purchase of office supplies is debited to the asset account Office Supplies, or it can be debited to the expense account Office Supplies Used. By means of an account for Office Supplies Used, or Expired Insurance, the adjustment can be made. This is an asset adjustment.

A liability adjustment is made similarly.

Adjusted Trial Balance

The trial balance summarizes only transactions during the accounting period. Insurance has expired, supplies have been used in operating the business, office and other salaries are incomplete, and equipment has depreciated. The adjustments must therefore be combined with trial-balance amounts by means of an adjusted trial balance.

Payroll

A good bookkeeping system must provide accurate information concerning the payroll. Because of Social Security laws, income tax withholding laws, and other state and federal regulations, any and all of this information must be instantly available. Therefore an Individual Payroll Record book should be maintained,

Information needed for accurate and complete accounting is listed on Form 40-A, supplied by the National Record Company:

1. Name of employee with address and personal data
2. Social Security number
3. Company number (if any)
4. Department number (if any)
5. Date employment began and ended (and reason for separation)
6. Dates worked, rate of pay, hours per day worked, regular and overtime status
7. Regular salaries paid if not on hourly basis
8. Deductions (Withholding Tax and Social Security)
9. Totals by month, quarter, and year.

XIV
The Plus Element

The closing chapter of this book can be brief because the most important instruction of all must come from the heart and the character of the secretary. She must apply all the rules to her daily experience in her own way; she must enlarge upon every possibility with the use of her own native intelligence.

In Elmer Rice's Broadway play, *Counsellor-at-Law*, starring Paul Muni, the role of his secretary was created by Anna Kostant. Because of her particular genius for portraying the devotion of a secretary, the audience saw a lyrical representation of the height of this vocation. With poise and the posture of self-reliance, erect and swift in her unobtrusive movements, she kept in rhythm with her employer, acting as automatically as his right hand, doing with the grace of a woman all that he wanted done and seeming to do it in anticipation of rather than as a result of his instructions.

It was an example of a secretary at the apex.

Every secretary who has taken to heart the suggestions contained in this *Manual* may herself attain that apex. Then with pride and pleasure in her work she will observe her employer's satisfaction that at last he has found the "right hand" he has always needed,

The National Secretaries Association, whose headquarters are at 1103 Grand Avenue, Kansas City, Missouri, has been granting certificates of CPS (Certified Professional Secretary) upon the successful completion of examinations in the various aspects of secretarial procedures and skills. Annually a board selects the "international boss of the year" as well as the "secretary of the year" for public awards. This recognition has helped to elevate the vocation in the business world's esteem. Serious secretaries may find it worthwhile to make inquiries about the activities of this association.